OUT OF

BABYLON

OUT OF

BABYLON

WALTER BRUEGGEMANN

ABINGDON PRESS
Nashville

OUT OF BABYLON

Copyright © 2010 by Abingdon Press

This book is printed on acid-free paper.

Library of Congress Cataloging-in-Publication Data

Brueggemann, Walter.
   Out of Babylon / Walter Brueggemann.
     p. cm.
   Includes bibliographical references (p.   ).
   ISBN 978-1-4267-1005-6 (trade pbk. : alk. paper)
   1. Christianity and culture—United States. 2. Imperialism—Biblical teaching. 3. Jews—History—Babylonian captivity, 598–515 B.C. 4. Babylonia—History—Religious aspects—Christianity. I. Title.

   BR517.B774 2010
   261.0973—dc22

                                     2010026843

10 11 12 13 14 15 16 17 18 19—10 9 8 7 6 5 4 3 2 1

MANUFACTURED IN THE UNITED STATES OF AMERICA

For
John Bracke

and in Memory of
David Knauert

CONTENTS

ACKNOWLEDGMENTS

I am glad to thank three stalwart colleagues at Abingdon Press. Judith Pierson, recently of Abingdon, had the initial idea and urging for a book extrapolated from the song "Time in Babylon." Bob Ratcliff has edited the manuscript vigorously, intensely, shrewdly, and with great care. John Kutsko, also recently of Abingdon, has been steadfast in seeing it through to completion and publication. To all three I am enormously indebted for their patient loyalty.

I am pleased to dedicate this book to John Bracke and to the memory of David Knauert. John Bracke was my first Old Testament student who has become a significant figure in the field and for a time my colleague at Eden Theological Seminary. He has been a steadfast witness for the evangelical pietism that is my spiritual home, and has served my alma mater with distinction. David Knauert was nearly the last of my Old Testament students. His early and untimely death cut much too short a grace-filled, well-lived life, and stopped at the outset his enormous promise as an Old Testament scholar. His absence will continue to be, for many of us, a hovering that fills us with gratitude and affection for him. Bracke and Knauert together roughly constitute bookends for my teaching years. As I name and ponder the distinguished succession of my students who have pursued Old Testament study, I am made aware in grateful ways what a blessed calling I have been privileged to practice.

Walter Brueggemann
Lent 2010

ABBREVIATIONS

BibInt	*Biblical Interpretation*
BZAW	Beihefte zur Zeitschrift für die alttestamentliche Wissenschaft
FOTL	Forms of the Old Testament Literature
JBL	*Journal of Biblical Literature*
JSOTSup	Journal for the Study of the Old Testament: Supplement Series
NIB	*The New Interpreter's Bible*
OBT	Overtures to Biblical Theology
OTL	Old Testament Library
PTMS	Pittsburgh Theological Monograph Series
SBLDS	Society of Biblical Literature Dissertation Series
SBLSymS	Society of Biblical Literature Symposium Series
SemeiaSt	Semeia Studies
WBC	Word Biblical Commentary

Five-lane highway danger zone
SUV and a speaker phone
You need that chrome to get you home
Doin' time in Babylon
Cluster mansion on the hill
Another day in Pleasantville
You don't like it take a pill
Doin' time in Babylon

In the land of the proud and free
You can sell your soul and your dignity
For fifteen minutes on TV
Doin' time in Babylon
So suck the fat, cut the bone
Fill it up with silicone
Everybody must get cloned
Doin' time in Babylon

Little Boy Blue come blow your horn
The crows are in the corn
The morning sky is red and falling down
The piper's at the till
He's coming for the kill
Luring all our children underground in Babylon

We came from apple pie and mom
Thru Civil Rights and Ban the Bomb
To Watergate and Vietnam
Hard times in Babylon
Rallied 'round the megaphone
Gave it up, just got stoned
Now it's Prada, Gucci and Perron
Doin' time in Babylon

Little Boy Blue come blow your horn
The crows are in the corn
The morning sky is red and falling down
The piper's at the till
He's coming for the kill
Luring all our children underground

Get results, get 'em fast
We're ready if you got the cash
Someone else will be laughin' last
Doin' time in Babylon
So put that conscience on the shelf
Keep the best stuff for yourself
Let the rest fight over what is left
Doin' time in Babylon

Little Boy Blue come blow your horn
The crows are in the corn
The morning sky is red and falling down
Let your song of healing spark
A way out of this dark
Lead us to a higher and a holy ground

CHAPTER 1

THE FACTS ON THE GROUND . . . TWICE!

> If I forget you, O Jerusalem,
> let my right hand wither!
> Let my tongue cling to the roof of my mouth,
> if I do not remember you,
> if I do not set Jerusalem above my highest joy.
>
> (Psalm 137:5-6)

These verses from the Psalter voice a passionate Jewish commitment that could not be silenced or nullified by the imperial power of Babylon. These verses succinctly encode the power relationship between the hegemony of Babylon and the defiant, pathos-filled resistance of Jews who continued to hold to their "local tradition" in spite of the power and requirements of the empire. In the discussion that follows, I will trace the defiant, pathos-filled resistance of "local truth" against empire, even as it continues among contemporary Christians who must live agilely in the midst of the deeply problematic power of the U.S. empire.

The great geopolitical fact for ancient Israel in the sixth century BCE was the Babylonian kingdom located in the Tigris-Euphrates Valley. To some extent the kingdom of Egypt to the south of Israel functioned in the sixth century, as it often did, as a counterweight to the great northern power. There is no doubt, however, that Babylon was the defining, generative power in international affairs, and so constituted an immediate threat to Israel. Babylon was a very ancient kingdom with advanced cultural and scientific learning. It experienced an important revival in the sixth century with the founding of a new dynasty. In the seventh century Babylon had been subordinated to the powerful kingdom of Assyria. But in 626 BCE Nabopolassar, together with important allies, broke free from Assyria, established an independent kingdom, and in twenty years displaced Assyria as the dominant regional power. In 605 he was succeeded on the throne by his son Nebuchadnezzar, who ruled until 562; the son brought the kingdom of Babylon to the apex of power and influence. The new dynasty presided over by two kings—father and son—had enormous expansionist ambitions, and so pushed relentlessly to the west. The dynasty came quickly to a sorry end through a series of ineffective leaders, culminating in the defeat of the kingdom at the hands of Cyrus, the rising Persian power to the east. Thus this Neo-Babylonian dynasty was only a brief episode in the long history of the ancient Near East.

For the Bible, however, the existence and aggressive military policies of Babylon constituted a defining moment in history—and therefore in faith—for ancient Israel. Babylon's military adventurism under Nebuchadnezzar inevitably led his armies to the Mediterranean Sea and inescapably toward Jerusalem and the state of Judah. Both the Bible and the cuneiform evidence left by the Babylonians indicate that Babylon undertook a series of military incursions into Judah, and three times came against the city of Jerusalem. It was, moreover, a policy of the Babylonians to reduce conquered peoples to acquiescent colonies by the stratagem of deporting the leadership class (who might have mounted resistance to such occupation) and relocating that elite population elsewhere.

The biblical evidence is terse.[1] But it indicates that Nebuchadnezzar besieged the city of Jerusalem in 598 BCE and carried away King Jehoiachin (2 Kings 24:10-12). In 587, moreover,

Nebuchadnezzar came again against the city and took away King Zedekiah, uncle of Jehoiachin (2 Kings 25:1-7). The narrative continues in order to report that Nebuzaradan, Nebuchadnezzar's general, carried into exile the rest of the people who were left in the city and the deserters who had defected to the king of Babylon—"all the rest of the population" (2 Kings 25:11). The following verse 12 concedes that the land was not left empty, but "some of the poorest people of the land," that is, the ones who could not initiate resistance to the empire, were left in the land (see also v. 14). The narrative of 2 Kings 25 reports that in these incursions the wealth of the temple plus all of the leading officers of the government were carried away, thus reducing the city and its population to impotence (2 Kings 24:13-16; 25:13-20).[2] These several verses trace the demise of Jerusalem's power and the culmination of the large narrative account of Israel in the land that began with the promise to Abraham and the occupation of the land by Joshua. The narrative is shaped in order to make clear that the Babylonian destruction of the city was an immense loss, bespeaking grief and humiliation. It was, moreover, an occurrence that required sustained interpretive attention in order to make sense of the crisis of culture and the crisis of faith. The evidence of the "facts on the ground" concerning the Babylonian destruction is not in doubt and is readily summarized. What remained, however, was an enormous interpretive task, a task that evoked Israel's best imagination that in turn resulted in the production of much of the material that now constitutes the Old Testament.[3]

It is not difficult to summarize these "facts on the ground." What requires careful attention, however, is the additional "fact on the ground" that the story told about these events amounted to a vigorous, sustained interpretation by a determined interpretive community. That community produced an ideological explanation that came to be constitutive for the ongoing community of Judaism. Among those Jews carried off to Babylon, a small, intentional, intense group seized the interpretive initiative and established the governing categories for how the destruction and deportation were to be understood. This cadre of interpreters opined about the *causes* of the destruction, the way of *coping* in the displacement, and the prospects for *ending* the displacement and *returning* home. All of which is only to say that the dominant narrative account of Jews in the sixth century is not an objective, disinterested report, but rather one that bears the ideological fingerprints of the group that created this particular interpretation of events that is appropriate to those who offer the interpretation. Perhaps inescapably, this account of the crisis of the sixth century draws all of its meaning close to this community of interpreters, that is, close to the deported elites in Babylon who understood and presented themselves as the faithful carriers and embodiment of true Israel into the future. That ideological force concluded:

- The destruction and deportation were the will and work of YHWH, whose Torah had been intolerably violated. Thus Nebuchadnezzar can be understood at most as a tool and agent of YHWH; or, as Jeremiah asserts, Nebuchadnezzar is YHWH's "servant" (Jeremiah 25:9; 27:6); the disaster is not simply a sociomilitary one; it is a theological disaster.
- It became the tenacious work of the community of Jews in Babylon to maintain this distinct identity as Jews, to practice the kind of Torah obedience that had not been practiced in Jerusalem, and to keep hope alive for the end of displacement and return to the land.

This simple narrative construction made theological sense and coherence out of a deeply incoherent historical experience. The story line offered by these Jews provided a theological *case* (punishment by YHWH) for Torah obedience, a *task* to practice Torah in a foreign land in order to maintain a holy people uncontaminated by alien context, and a *hope* for return home. The sequence of *case, task,* and *hope* is reflected in the tenacious insistence of

Psalm 137, a song of the deportees that keeps the energy of the community sharply focused on Jerusalem:

> By the rivers of Babylon—
>   there we sat down and there we wept,
>   when we remembered Zion. . . .
> If I forget you, O Jerusalem,
>   let my right hand wither!
> Let my tongue cling to the roof of my mouth,
>   if I do not remember you,
>   if I do not set Jerusalem above my highest joy.
>
> (Psalm 137:1, 5-6)

The song freely acknowledged life in an alien context, but refused to accommodate that life at all. In the end the psalm voices profound hostility against all things Babylonian, the violent rage that is voiced being a function of hope that is lodged in a distinct identity that refused any imperial accommodation:

> O daughter Babylon, you devastator!
>   Happy shall they be who pay you back
>   what you have done to us!
> Happy shall they be who take your little ones
>   and dash them against the rock! (vv. 8-9)

It is this tenacity that gives Judaism such staying power. And it is the deep fissure of this sixth-century disaster that has given Judaism its primary form, so much so that Jacob Neusner can judge that the theme of *exile and return* has become paradigmatic for all Jews for all time to come:

The vast majority of the nation did not undergo the experiences of exile and return. One part never left, the other never came back. That fact shows us the true character of the Judaism that would predominate: it began by making a selection of facts to be deemed consequential, hence historical, and by ignoring, in the making of that selection, the experience of others who had a quite different appreciation of what had happened—and, for all we know, a different appreciation of the message. For, after all, the Judeans who did not go into exile also did not rebuild the temple, and the ones in Babylonia did not try.[4]

YHWH is the one who willed the deportation; Babylon is the agent who enacted that deportation. This assignment of roles to YHWH and to Babylon was accomplished through a daring interpretive maneuver that imposed a certain logic upon events, a logic rooted in the covenantal nomism of the tradition of Deuteronomy, wherein Torah obedience or disobedience will variously yield blessings and curses. The disaster of the sixth century, so goes the paradigm, was a justly merited curse worked against those who had violated covenantal obedience. This logic both imposed meaning on chaotic events and established the voice of the deported elite as normative for the larger community.

But since we are here concerned with "facts on the ground," we must pause to notice that there is an important dissonance between the facts on the ground and this normative construction of historical reality. Neusner puts it this way:

> Because the Mosaic Torah's interpretation of the diverse experiences of the Israelites after the destruction of the Temple in 586 invoked—whether pertinent or not—the categories of exile and return, so constructing as paradigmatic the experience of only a minority of the families of the Jews (most in Babylonia stayed there, many in the Land of Israel never left), through the formation of the Pentateuch, the Five Books of Moses, the events from 586 to 450 B.C., became for all time to come the generative and definitive pattern of meaning. Consequently, whether or not the paradigm precipitated dissonance with their actual circumstance, Jews in diverse settings have constructed their worlds, that is, shaped their identifications, in accord with that one, generative model. They therefore have perpetually rehearsed that human experience imagined by the original priestly authorship of the Torah in the time of Ezra. . . . To state the matter simply, the

paradigm that imparted its imprint on the history of the day did not emerge from, was not generated by, the events of the age. First came the system, its world-view and the way of life formed whole we know not where or by whom. Then came the selection, by the system, of consequential events and their patterning into systemic propositions. And finally, at a third stage (of indeterminate length of time) came the formation and composition of the canon that would express the logic of the system and state those "events" that the system would select or invent for its own expression.[5]

Neusner deduces two historical realities to which we may add a third:

• Many in the land of Israel never left. It is now a commonplace of scholarship that the land was never empty; there was a functioning community remaining in the land that the Babylonians did not bother to eliminate. Thus Jeremiah 41:3-5 indicates that worship continued at the temple site in Jerusalem.
• Most of those deported from Jerusalem to Babylon remained in Babylon. The evidence is that many of the deported Jews came to play a prominent role in the ongoing economic life of Babylon, and managed to sustain Jewish identity while participating in the imperial economy. Only a small number of scribal-priestly fanatics were committed to "return."
• Babylon continued to be an important, even defining socioeconomic, political force for all in the region, a force that could not be disregarded.

The defining importance of Babylon is made clear enough in the tradition of Jeremiah. In the initial poetry of the book, there is an ominous "foe from the North" anticipated by the poet who remains unnamed, but is surely Babylon (Jeremiah 1:11-14; 5:14-17).[6] More explicitly, the prose of Jeremiah names

Nebuchadnezzar as "my servant" (Jeremiah 25:9; 27:6), who is authorized and empowered to enact the devastation of Judaism that is willed by YHWH. In these texts Babylon is viewed as a dangerous and inescapable threat to the city.

The book of Jeremiah gives voice to a small group of figures clustered around the prophet who believed that the royal policies in Jerusalem were quite wrong.[7] The advocacy of this group, surely grounded in political realism, insisted that Jerusalem surrender to Babylon rather than be destroyed. A theological version of this advocacy—that went hand in glove with this political judgment—is that YHWH willed the triumph of Babylon, and that it was senseless and disobedient to resist the empire. The leading advocate in the tradition is Shaphan, whose son is also prominent in the tradition and whose grandson, Gedaliah, is appointed as a trusted governor of the province by the Babylonians after the defeat of the monarchy.[8]

Three texts in Jeremiah in particular counsel accommodation to Babylon, a political realism that is given theological formulation. First and best known, in his famous "letter to the exiles," Jeremiah encourages the deported to "seek the welfare of the city where I have sent you into exile, and pray to the LORD on its behalf, for in its welfare you will find your welfare" (Jeremiah 29:7).

More than simply accommodating Babylon, this text urges coming to terms with the empire as the unavoidable matrix for Jewish well-being. Deported Jews must come to terms with Babylon! Second, in Jeremiah 38:17 the tradition exhibits the prophet urging surrender to Babylon as a way to save the city: "If you will only surrender to the officials of the king of Babylon, then your life shall be spared, and this city shall not be burned with fire, and you and your house shall live."

And third, awkwardly, in Jeremiah 42:11-12, the prophet urges reliance on the mercy of Babylon as an expression of YHWH's own mercy:

> Do not be afraid of the king of Babylon, as you have been; do
> not be afraid of him, says the LORD, for I am with you, to save
> you and to rescue you from his hand. I will grant you mercy,
> and he will have mercy on you and restore you to your native
> soil.

Here the tradition anticipates "mercy" from the very kingdom that
it earlier said would "have no mercy" (Jeremiah 6:23).

In this rendering of reality, YHWH is the ultimate actor. It is
YHWH who will "pluck up" and "pull down," who will "build
and . . . plant" (Jeremiah 1:10). But second to YHWH, Babylon is
the main player, who moves harshly against Jerusalem, and who
will host the venue . . . on this reading . . . for whatever may appear
next on the Jewish horizon.

Clearly, Babylon comes to occupy a role of enormous importance
in Jewish imagination. It is Babylon that destroyed and deported; it
is Babylon that becomes (for now) a venue for shalom; and it is
Babylon from which the most tenacious Jews intend to depart.[9]

What follows in this book is a sustained reflection on Babylon in
faithful imagination, first for Jews and derivatively for Christians.
Within the Old Testament, Babylon occupies a central position in
what it means to be Jewish. In the Old Testament, the imagining of
Babylon is inescapably from the perspective of Jewishness. To start
with, Jews perceive Babylon as threat, but then Babylon is also recognized as a viable venue for faithfulness over a long period of
time:

> Build houses and live in them; plant gardens and eat what
> they produce. Take wives and have sons and daughters; take
> wives for your sons, and give your daughters in marriage,
> that they may bear sons and daughters; multiply there, and
> do not decrease. (Jeremiah 29:5-6)

And for some Jews not of the tenacious variety, Babylon became a
homeland in which Jewish identity could be practiced, albeit with
all sorts of inevitable compromises.

Completely apart from its relation to Jewish life, Babylon was a hegemonic power whose goal was to be all-defining for life in the world. It is the work of such hegemonic power (empire) to exercise total governmental control and, where possible, total economic and cultural control as well.[10] Empires like Babylon lack both patience and tolerance toward those whose ultimate loyalty belongs to someone or something other than the empire itself. In response to such resistant loyalties, the empire will move beyond total control into totalitarian "final solutions."[11]

Viewed from the "localism" of a competing loyalty among Jews, Babylon may become an unwelcome venue for faith. The poems concerning Babylon in Isaiah 13 and Jeremiah 50–51 portray a ruthless power of enormous arrogance that in the long run cannot be sustained.[12] That arrogance is characteristically articulated as a menacing imposition upon the local population, and was understood as a challenge to the rule of God. If one were a Babylonian, however, the empire's success would have been the source of an uncommon deposit of wealth, privilege, and entitlement guaranteed by the military agency of Babylon, an agency that ensured a reliable flow of capital to the city. Faith in YHWH recognized the illusionary nature of the empire's claim to ultimacy. Such recognition, on the lips of Jews, served to keep Babylonian hegemony penultimate, a conviction given in the formulation of Daniel: "until you have learned that the Most High has sovereignty over the kingdom of mortals, and gives it to whom he will" (Daniel 4:25, 32).

But the Babylonians themselves would have found the privileges and gifts of empire wondrous to receive and, in the end, perhaps "our just due." Thus we may imagine that the passionate protests and alternative hopes of the faith of Jews sustained a counterview of history. At the same time, however, the attractions of Babylon were powerful indeed. Surely many Jews, in Babylon as well as back in Jerusalem, sought ways to come to terms with Babylonian reality. Shaphan was a political leader and Jeremiah was a covenantal voice that tilted toward accommodation to the empire that does not, according to their own lights, give too much away.

Our chapter title says "twice," *twice* a hegemonic empire; *twice* a set of loyalties that challenged the empire's claims of ultimacy; twice a context of accommodation, resistance, and alternative. It is no new thing to suggest that the contemporary United States mirrors ancient Babylon in its totalizing propensity. To be sure, between Babylon and the United States there appear a well-known series of totalizing powers, notably Rome and Spain, the Netherlands, and England in the modern world.[13] Our study here, however, without denying the significance of the hegemonic powers that came between, links Babylon and the United States because Babylon has metaphorical force in the ongoing theological tradition and because the United States is our current context and venue for accommodation, resistance, and alternative. There are, of course, no easy or obvious or exact moves from "then" to "now," and the parallels are necessarily imaginative, impressionistic, and inexact.

Nonetheless, the study of such a linkage is an enterprise worth pursuing, because our own situation of empire in the United States matters enormously to all those with alternative loyalties, especially people with "local traditions of faith."[14] Christians in the United States are accustomed to read the Bible in a democratic context where we have political-religious freedom guaranteed by the Constitution or, even more, to read the Bible with the United States cast in the role of God's chosen people and carrier of God's will for freedom in the world, an exceptionalism that pervades our public discourse.[15] Such a reading becomes a very difficult matter, however, when the facts on the ground exhibit the United States as empire, as the place for faithful reading and faithful living according to an alternative loyalty that is in deep tension with the totalizing claims of empire.[16]

In order to take into account our inescapable contemporary venue for faithful Bible reading, it is important to consider the fact on the ground of the United States as empire, and to consider the analogue to how Babylon is imagined in Scripture. The United States has been a long time under way in becoming empire, perhaps partly by accident, perhaps by militant intention, and partly, if we may say so, by divine purpose. From the outset the United States has dreamed large and powerfully:

- Already in the Monroe Doctrine the U.S. government staked out an enormous territorial claim, a claim much larger than its capacity to control it.

- It is commonly understood that the Spanish-American War of 1898 was the beginning of the overt territorial expansionism of the United States, though one could as well argue that the western movement under James K. Polk was already an aggressive act of preemption.

- From the McKinley war of 1898 came Theodore Roosevelt with his assertive claims for U.S. greatness. There is a direct line, moreover, from Roosevelt and his secretary of state, Elihu Root, to the expansionism of the twentieth century under those tutored by Henry Stimson, those who became "The Wise Men" of the twentieth century.[17]

- The agreements at Yalta that secretly divided the world into a U.S.-dominated West and the Soviet Union, a division tilted soon after by the U.S. possession (and dropping) of the atomic bombs, make clear the intentions of the power brokers of U.S. policy, epitomized by the memo of Paul Nitze and the "containment" thesis of George Kennan.[18]

- The collapse of the Soviet Union, perhaps hastened by the United States in its strong intransigence, sealed the deal for U.S. domination on the world scene.[19]

- And now, belatedly, in the reach of the neoconservatives in Iraq, we are able to see the shameless aggressiveness of the United States in every direction, so that "national interest" has evolved into domination.

Now my purpose is not to trace U.S. territorial ambition or expansion. It is rather to ponder what has happened to the self-perception and self-understanding of U.S. citizens who are the beneficiaries of this march toward global control, beneficiaries whether as zealous supporters of U.S. aggressiveness or even as reluctant dissenters. Either way, U.S. citizens have benefited enormously as U.S. culture and language have become increasingly dominant all around the world.

The emergence of the United States as empire has pivoted on its point of unrivaled military advantage. But U.S. military advantage was and is closely tied to U.S. economic leverage, so that the U.S. flag, without any precise formulation, has come to symbolize both a powerful military commitment and an aggressive capitalism that is endlessly in pursuit of new markets and natural resources.[20] All of this, moreover, has been intimately tied to "the Bible," so that there is missional fervor and rationale for the imposition of U.S. cultural domination in the world. Indeed, much of the missional energy of the U.S. church carried with it the U.S. flag and U.S. dollars, so that it has become very difficult to sort out what, in such missional efforts, belongs to Caesar and what belongs to God. The outcome has been an unprecedented accumulation of power, influence, and leverage in the world, with enormous benefit to the United States in terms of a seemingly limitless standard of living.

I propose this parallel between ancient Babylon and the contemporary United States in order to ask a question: is this sense of privilege and entitlement, bolstered by an uncritical joining of Bible and flag and underwritten by military and economic dominance, a proper legacy to leave coming generations in the United States? I ask this question cognizant of the fact that political discourse in the United States, in a variety of modes, is essentially a conversation about how to sustain this "God-given" advantage in the world. I say this, fully mindful of evidence of dissenting reality:

- 9/11 was a savage protest against such hegemony.
- The crisis of global warming, now beyond contestation,

13

indicates that this "unnatural" standard of living cannot be sustained. (The food crisis evoked by the diversion of corn for ethanol alerts us to the delicate balance of haves and have-nots in the world).

- The rise of Islam into world politics calls attention to the diminished supply of fossil fuels and evokes awareness of "oil wars," past and in time to come.

- The rise of the Chinese economy is a large challenge to the U.S. hegemony.

The signs of challenge to the present hegemony are everywhere.[21] Empires rarely notice such challenge in time, nor do they concede anything to those who mount the challenge. Thus the prospect, as with Babylon until Cyrus the Persian arrived, is that the U.S. sense of entitlement and control will continue to drive public discourse and policy formation long after the facts on the ground indicate otherwise.

The following discussion proceeds with the suggestion that the glory of ancient Babylon and the resolve of the contemporary United States is a clear enough parallel that the case of Babylon can be instructive for us. Both empires are to be seen for what they are. In the case of Babylon, however, our interest is of a peculiar kind, namely, to consider how it was for Jews to live in the midst of such empire, to take seriously the imperial facts on the ground, and yet to sustain a distinctive "local identity." By "local identity" in this case I mean the Jewish sense of belonging peculiarly to the God of covenant and committed publicly to the practice of Torah. The challenge must have been different for different segments of the Jewish community, those remaining in the land of Israel and those deported to Babylon. But for all of them, the challenge of "local identity" was a demanding one in the face of empire that programmatically was impatient with and intolerant of local tradition whenever it contradicted imperial intention.

As the Jews in the Babylonian Empire had to struggle with the seductions and insistences of empire, so Christians in the midst of U.S. empire must struggle for peculiar identity. The tradition of Deuteronomy worried that prosperity would produce amnesia, so that the "local tradition" of emancipation would be forgotten in the face of newly granted entitlements:

> When the LORD your God has brought you into the land that he swore to your ancestors, to Abraham, to Isaac, and to Jacob, to give you—a land with fine, large cities that you did not build, houses filled with all sorts of goods that you did not fill, hewn cisterns that you did not hew, vineyards and olive groves that you did not plant—and when you have eaten your fill, take care that you do not forget the LORD, who brought you out of the land of Egypt, out of the house of slavery. (Deuteronomy 6:10-12)

> The LORD your God is bringing you into a good land, a land with flowing streams, with springs and underground waters welling up in valleys and hills, a land of wheat and barley, of vines and fig trees and pomegranates, a land of olive trees and honey, a land where you may eat bread without scarcity, where you will lack nothing, a land whose stones are iron and from whose hills you may mine copper. You shall eat your fill and bless the LORD your God for the good land that he has given you.
>
> Take care that you do not forget the LORD your God, by failing to keep his commandments, his ordinances, and his statutes, which I am commanding you today. When you have eaten your fill and have built fine houses and live in them, and when your herds and flocks have multiplied, and your silver and gold is multiplied, and all that you have is multiplied, then do not exalt yourself, forgetting the LORD your God, who brought you out of the land of Egypt, out of the house of slavery. . . . Do not say to yourself, "My power and the might of my own hand have gotten me this wealth." (Deuteronomy 8:7-14, 17)

Mutatis mutandis, amid the limitless prosperity of the U.S. economy (an expectation when not a fact), it is profoundly problematic to hold to a tradition that features sacrifice for the sake of holiness and justice for the sake of the neighbor. Life in Babylon constituted a demanding work of agility among the adherents of this "local tradition." That tradition attests, always again, to another belonging, another loyalty, and another citizenship. Empire, however, allows no rivals and no competitors. One can sense the dismissive impatience for any "hyphenated American" who remembers another belonging, and a rude intolerance for those who cherish a "mother tongue" other than the language of the empire. Indeed, the empire is impatient with those who embody any trace of "other," for the presence of "other" exposes the empire's claim of ultimacy as false or at least compromised. "Local tradition," however, is always about "other." Consequently, the Jews in ancient Babylon struggled over their otherness. And the struggle in the U.S. empire—among Christians—is not to be finished any time soon. There may be more than one strategy for that struggle; by whatever name, it is an urgent and demanding issue among us.

CHAPTER 2

Awaiting Babylon

> The LORD warned Israel and Judah by every prophet and every seer, saying, "Turn from your evil ways and keep my commandments and my statutes, in accordance with all the law that I commanded your ancestors and that I sent to you by my servants the prophets." They would not listen but were stubborn, as their ancestors had been, who did not believe in the LORD their God. They despised his statutes, and his covenant that he made with their ancestors, and the warnings that he gave them. They went after false idols and became false; they followed the nations that were around them, concerning whom the LORD had commanded them that they should not do as they did. (2 Kings 17:13-15)

The Babylonian incursion into Jerusalem that had triggered the exile did not need to have come upon the city as a surprise. The entire prophetic tradition that has been sounding for two centuries had warned Jerusalem about the risks of covenantal disobedience and had anticipated the summary judgment of YHWH against such recalcitrance. The entire prophetic literature is to be understood as a sustained summons to Israel to repent and return to Torah obedience. Israel, however, was hard-hearted and confident of its own destiny in the world, and consistently refused to heed the poets.

In a parallel way, the United States as empire has had a long tradition of summoning poetic voices that have warned about socioeconomic exploitation and political injustice. The list of such
poetic, prophetic utterers out beyond imperial categories is long
and honored. Contemporary voices that belong to such a risky
honor include Martin Luther King, Jr., Daniel Berrigan, Michael
Lerner, William Sloane Coffin, William Stringfellow, Jim Wallis,
Jim Forbes, Gordon Cosby, Will Campbell, and many others readily named. Like that ancient empire, however, the United States
empire, living in a cocoon of self-justification, has been largely
immune to such warning.

Thus, in both ancient and contemporary settings, the interface
between empire and divine purpose is carried by poetic, prophetic
voices that arise from and are nurtured by the "local tradition" of
faith. As in the ancient world, the contemporary abrasion between
imperial ideology and poetic alternative is a contentious one, with
the poetic alternative being fragile and mostly unauthorized and
unrecognized.

The idea of empire is writ large in the Old Testament.[1] The paradigmatic narrative of Moses begins in empire, that of Pharaoh.
Pharaoh fully embodies his empire, ruthlessly placing the needs of
production over those of human beings and holding himself
accountable to nothing and to no one. But then, so the story goes,
Moses and Aaron led the slave community out of the coercive productivity of the empire, and Pharaoh was helpless to hold them.
The Exodus narrative reports the limit of the empire in the face of
human groan and holy hope. The story speaks of the hope of the
slaves, the capacity of YHWH to "get glory," and the pitiful impotence of Pharaoh (Exodus 14:4, 17).

The slave community proceeded, in fits and starts, through the
wilderness to Sinai, the venue for the construction, formulation,
and embrace of Israel's "local tradition." Thus "local tradition"
looks at the world differently than the empire; it tells an alternative
and opposing story to that of empire centered on the covenant with

YHWH. This local tradition is joined to the memory of empire by its opposition to the empire: "I am the LORD your God, who brought you out of the land of Egypt, out of the house of slavery" (Exodus 20:2). YHWH is the decisive agent for departure (Exodus) from the empire.

It is remarkable that after that encounter at Sinai, the empire appears little on the horizon of the Moses-Sinai narrative.[2] For the most part it is the departure from and alternative to empire that preoccupies Israel as it builds its local tradition. YHWH's summons and instruction to Moses focuses sharply on Israel's status as a chosen people. That chosenness sets Israel apart from the nations, and certainly from the seductions of empire:

> You are a people holy to the LORD your God; the LORD your God has chosen you out of all the peoples on earth to be his people, his treasured possession. It was not because you were more numerous than any other people that the LORD set his heart on you and chose you—for you were the fewest of all peoples. It was because the LORD loved you and kept the oath that he swore to your ancestors, that the LORD has brought you out with a mighty hand, and redeemed you from the house of slavery, from the hand of Pharaoh king of Egypt. (Deuteronomy 7:6-8; see 10:14-15; 14:2)

Before long, of course, Israel reentered the world of the nations. Its mandate as a different people could not exist in a vacuum, but only in the real world. But being different in the real world created new desire in Israel to forgo its distinctiveness: "Appoint for us, then, a king to govern us, like other nations. . . . No! but we are determined to have a king over us, so that we also may be like other nations, and that our king may govern us and go out before us and fight our battles" (1 Samuel 8:5, 19-20).

And so the issue is joined that has vexed God's chosen people ever since. Those who told Israel's story rejected the desire to name a king and be like the other nations. They took little notice of empire, and cringed when Solomon tried to create an empire in

Israel, notably by using forced (slave) labor. They saw Solomon as Pharaoh reborn, empire déjà vu.[3] The story they told had little room for seeing Israel as an empire; it was too focused on Israel's difference and otherness from the nations, especially from the empire.[4]

It remained for the prophets to bring Israel and empire into the same horizon. While deeply rooted in Israel's distinctive covenant with YHWH, they are also fully aware of the "real world" events unfolding around them. They give us a theological read of the real world, making the empire part of the story of YHWH's covenant with Israel. The move from the normative covenantal tradition to prophetic imagination is a huge one, one that bears decisively on our theme of empire and "local tradition."[5] There is no doubt that the prophets are fully preoccupied with the "local tradition" of covenant. But they do the hard work of situating "local tradition" in the world of empire by asking, "What is the meaning and role of empire, seen in the light of God's covenant with Israel?" They do not ask about empire from the large perspective of world history or from the perspective of the empire itself. Rather, they ask from the standpoint of the covenant. That is, they do not read "top down" from empire to "local tradition," but "bottom up" from "local tradition" to empire. This peculiar reading assigns to the empire a place it would never have assigned (or even imagined for) itself: a participant in the larger story of YHWH's rule, a rule that Klaus Koch calls "meta-history."[6] That is, there is more and other going on in the world of public politics than the empire was able to imagine. It is that "more" and "other" that preoccupied the prophets and that rendered the empire, against its own self-perception, as decidedly secondary in the life of the world.

Here I will call attention to five prophetic voices that are typical and representative of the way in which empire is rendered important but secondary in the horizon of this "local tradition."

AMOS

Amos, reckoned to be the first in Israel of these poetic voices, lived and spoke at a time when the Assyrian Empire had not yet come to new aggressive forcefulness. We may learn from Amos most of what we need to know about empire in prophetic imagination. Amos speaks of an unnamed threat to Israel. It is likely that he performed his utterance before his contemporaries recognized Assyria as a major threat. Even though Amos does not mention Assyria by name, he clearly has Assyria in mind. In 4:2-3, after indicting Israel for greed and exploitation, he avers:

> The Lord GOD has sworn by his holiness:
>> The time is surely coming upon you,
> when they shall take you away with hooks,
>> even the last of you with fishhooks.
> Through breaches in the wall you shall leave,
>> each one straight ahead;
>> and you shall be flung out into Harmon.

The "they" that is to come is not named, but it is the menacing empire. The threat, moreover, is to be "flung out," for Amos knew about the practice of deportation executed by the Assyrians, whom the Babylonians subsequently imitated. Chapter 4 verses 1-3 links the covenantal *failure of Israel to* the coming *threat of empire.* This juxtaposition recurs in the Prophets and is an extraordinary interpretive maneuver each time it occurs. It connects *covenantal failure* and *foreign incursion*, a connection made possible by the rule and intention of YHWH. When the empire came against Israel (as it surely did), there were ample "real world" explanations for why they did so. The prophets characteristically refuse such explanations and choose, instead, to give the imperial onslaught a theological grounding. Empires work, so say the poets, at the behest of YHWH to enforce and enact faithfulness to the covenant. Thus when the prophet sees the failure and dysfunction of his society, he

21

can only await empire, for he knows the connection wrought in the resolve of YHWH.

The strategic decision of Amos to leave the threat unnamed and unidentified only adds to its ominous quality. We can see the same strategy in Amos 4:12, where the threat is left only as "thus, this," whereby Israel is to "meet your God" in the public affairs of history. The ground for such a threat, in this interpretation, is that Israel has refused its own true character. Rather than ordering its life according to YHWH's will, it has arranged its economy in exploitative and anti-neighborly ways. This is made more explicit in the indictment of 6:4-6. In its self-indulgent greed, Israel has ceased to have a future *as* Israel. Even more sobering, it has failed to notice its own demise or to grieve its failure. Its practice of an indulgent life has dulled its capacity for self-awareness. The inevitable outcome of such obtuseness, says the poet, is exile (v. 7). Again the prophet alludes to standard imperial practice and imagines, well ahead of events, that Israel will be subject to that policy precisely because it has betrayed its true identity and character.

It is clear Amos's words pertain to the Assyrian threat. Babylon is not yet on the horizon, and so Amos remains remote from our topic of study, the Babylonians. His utterance matters for us, however, on two counts. First, there is no doubt that the northern utterance of Amos concerning Assyria was reused a century later in Judah, now with reference to Babylon. Thus, for example, the oracle concerning Judah in Amos 2:4-5 anticipates "fire" and "devour[ing]" that are surely to be understood with reference to Babylon. But second and more important, all empires act the same way; all empires are self-indulgent, arrogant, and abusive. For that reason, it does not matter that Amos spoke with reference to Assyria, for the poetry can be readily recycled and read into the world of Babylon—which it was—without changing a syllable. Empire is empire, and the prophet can imagine empire at the behest of YHWH. His listeners only had to wait. And they would see!

MICAH

Micah, a later southern contemporary of Amos, also has Assyria in purview. In 2:1-2 Micah criticizes the aggressive acquisitiveness of the economic managers of Judah. And in verse 3, he has YHWH declare: "I am devising against this family an evil."

The verb *devise* is not a verb of action. The action will not be done by YHWH but by a historical agent whom YHWH has authorized to act. Again, while the threat is unnamed, it is, clearly, a concrete historical threat; the reference to "our captors" in verse 4 surely alludes to the coming Assyrian army.[7] Like Amos, Micah understands that the chosen people are under threat from a specific military power, but a power summoned by YHWH in response to violation of YHWH's will and purpose. Micah can envision a time when the conqueror of the land will reassign property lines and the perpetrators of the violations will be excluded from the redeployment of land. The theological underpinning is given quite concrete socioeconomic implementation.

ISAIAH

The matter is not different for Isaiah, whose work pertains to the Assyrian period. In 5:25-30, after a series of "woes" (vv. 8-23), the prophet voices the anger of YHWH against Israel:

> The anger of the Lord was kindled against his people,
>   and he stretched out his hand against them and
>   struck them;
>   the mountains quaked, and their corpses were like refuse
>   in the streets.
> For all this his anger has not turned away,
>   and his hand is stretched out still. (Isaiah 5:25)

But that anger is not enacted directly. The poet entertains no simplistic supernaturalism. Rather, as YHWH "devised" in Micah 2:3, so here YHWH will only "raise a signal . . . and whistle for" (v. 26) an invading people.[8] The poet moves easily from the anger of YHWH in verse 25 to the arrows and bows and horses and wheels of a coming army that will groan and seize and carry off and roar. Empire, in this poetic instance, is to be an "enforcer" for YHWH. In 10:5-6, the poetry becomes more explicit. Now it is Assyria by name. It is empire as "rod" and "club" of YHWH. It is empire dispatched "against a godless nation," that is, against YHWH's own people. The vocation of empire in prophetic horizon is to assert YHWH's rule. Indeed, YHWH chooses to enhance and empower empire. "But . . . ," says the poet, "but . . ." (v. 7). The first endorsement of empire in verses 5-6 is immediately qualified, if not retracted. Assyria cannot live by YHWH's mandate:

> *But* this is not what he intends,
>   nor does he have this in mind;
> *but* it is in his heart to destroy,
>   and to cut off nations not a few.
> (Isaiah 10:7, emphasis added)

Assyria's intent is more aggressive than YHWH's. Assyria cannot restrain its aggressive acquisitiveness. It cannot limit its brutality, even if it is YHWH-authorized brutality. In verses 5-7 we are able to see the mature prophetic understanding of empire, which is seen to be a vehicle for divine purpose, but seen also to violate divine purpose in arrogant self-assertion. The empire is, simultaneously, vehicle and violator! The prophets know that empires in very short order enact arrogance and imagine themselves autonomous and not accountable to YHWH. Thus the imagined rhetoric of the haughty Assyrian king in verses 13-14 is filled with unqualified first person pronouns that reflect excessive assertiveness and unrestrained pride and boastfulness. By verse 16, the poetry of Isaiah reverses field; YHWH turns against a rapacious power that refused a God-given mandate. Isaiah is expecting Assyria; but chapter 39 asserts that the naive king had invited Babylon into the primary state secrets. Not only is Babylon awaited in the book of Isaiah; it is invited in! The Jerusalem king is prepared to play the imperial game . . . and will lose!

JEREMIAH

A century later, as the demise of Jerusalem seemed imminent and as Babylonian power grew strong and threatening, the prophet Jeremiah reiterated, with reference to Babylon, what his prophetic predecessors had said about Assyria. In his call narrative, after receiving a remarkable mandate from YHWH (1:10), the poet receives two visions granted him by YHWH. In the second vision he is given to see "a boiling pot, tilted away from the north" (v. 13). In the geopolitics of the Old Testament, the "boiling pot" of trouble and threat is always from the north. In Jeremiah's time it is Babylon, but it is Babylon left unnamed and ominous in the absence of specificity. It is "out of the north" that "evil" (=disaster) will break out (v. 14). It is, moreover, a northern evil that "I am calling" (v. 15). Again it is empire at the behest of YHWH because in prophetic imagination it is YHWH who has the whole world in his hands, has the empire in his hands, and dispatches empires to do the alien work of punishment.

In chapters 4–6 Jeremiah offers a series of poems about the coming of an invasive imperial power. This anticipated threat is unmistakably Babylon, a threat that will remain unnamed until chapter 20.[9] Leaving the threat unidentified is part of the poetic strategy of dread. By chapter 4, Jeremiah has established the infidelity of Israel toward YHWH; now it is all about the moral coherence of public history, whereby historical threat is seen to be a divine response to theological infidelity. One cannot read this poetry without being constantly impressed with the daring imagination that can deliver imperial threat in response to the violations of this little people Israel. The entire landscape of public history is mobilized around the crisis in Jerusalem, even if the superpower of the day in fact took almost no notice of what had transpired in Jerusalem.[10]

What a threat this poet can anticipate! The empire is like a waiting lion, a wolf, a leopard:

> A lion from the forest shall kill them,
>   a wolf from the desert shall destroy them.
> A leopard is watching against their cities;
>   everyone who goes out of them shall be torn in pieces—
> because their transgressions are many,
>   their apostasies are great. (Jeremiah 5:6)

The empire is on the face of it ancient, enduring, mysterious, huge, devouring:

> It is an enduring nation,
>   it is an ancient nation,
> a nation whose language you do not know,
>   nor can you understand what they say.
> Their quiver is like an open tomb;
>   all of them are mighty warriors.
> They shall eat up your harvest and your food;
>   they shall eat up your sons and your daughters;
> they shall eat up your flocks and your herds;
>   they shall eat up your vines and your fig trees;
> they shall destroy with the sword
>   your fortified cities in which you trust. (5:15-17)

The empire is loud, boisterous, unrestrained . . . without mercy:

> See, a people is coming from the land of the north,
>   a great nation is stirring from the farthest parts
>   of the earth.
> They grasp the bow and the javelin,
>   they are cruel and have no mercy,
>   their sound is like the roaring sea;
> they ride on horses,
>   equipped like a warrior for battle,
>   against you, O daughter Zion! (6:22-23)

This is the way of empire, always, everywhere. It will happen here . . . and there is no escape, no alternative.

It remained for the prose tradition of Jeremiah to make the poetry specific and concrete. The prose gets precise about negotiations, options, and the threat faced by Jerusalem. But the prose is not required in order to sense the dread that is deep and ferocious and inescapable. The empire is coming! Nebuchadnezzar is coming! He is, moreover, coming at the behest of YHWH, for he is the "servant" of YHWH (25:9; 27:6). It is no wonder that the king in Jerusalem hoped for a "wonderful deed" by YHWH in the face of empire (21:2). The local tradition is rooted in miracles, and now is an urgent time for one. But there is to be no miracle of deliverance; there could not be, so say the prophets, because the people of the local tradition had forfeited that possibility in their recalcitrance.

ZEPHANIAH

I mention Zephaniah, contemporary of Jeremiah, only to notice a contrasting mode of speech. In Zephaniah as in Jeremiah, the city is under acute threat. But remarkably, Zephaniah allows for no human agent in the threat. It is all YHWH, directly and relentlessly. Thus the poetry of 1:2-4 is dominated by first person pronouns. YHWH is the single agent who matters. While Zephaniah's intent is the same as Jeremiah's—to assert that the empire will do all the heavy lifting in the divine assault on Jerusalem—this passage leaves no room for human agency. To this extent, the rhetoric of Zephaniah is that much disconnected from the political reality of the city. But as in all good poetry, much is left unsaid that is heard anyway.

We are able to see from this sampling of texts that the prophetic tradition in the eighth and seventh centuries consistently situates the chosen people in the path of empire, and shows the local tradition at acute risk from the empire's hegemonic power. That in itself is a fair reading of geopolitical reality, for great powers are always devouring smaller powers. What is peculiar—and problematic—is the theological dimension of the threat on which the prophets insist. This is not simply Assyria or Babylon on the march. YHWH instigates the action! Thus the prophets, by force of rhetoric, take the scars and ashes and dread of human history and find in them moral, theological coherence. Empires have their penultimate work to do vis-à-vis local tradition, even vis-à-vis God's own preferred partner and subject. The preferred rhetoric to which the prophets repeatedly return is a *speech of judgment* in which *internal failure* evokes *external threat*, the connection between them assured by the will and resolve of YHWH.[11] The whole of geopolitics is taken as a force field for obedience, justice, and holiness.

We need to look at this picture of empire and local tradition from two vantage points. First and most obviously, we consider it with reference to ancient reality, a reading in which the contours of interpretation are clear enough. The prophets overlay this reading upon the "facts" of Israel's and Judah's encounter with the ancient empires we have discussed. But we look twice, the second time with reference to our own imperial time and place.

When we consider *empire and local tradition* with reference to the United States, we need to understand that it can be seen as filling both roles. Many in the history of the United States have understood it to carry the "local tradition" of a special covenant relationship to God. At the same time, is there a better modern-day candidate to occupy the role of empire? This double reading is necessary because there is no obvious equivalent between ancient reading and contemporary setting. If, however, we take the biblical rendering as in some way relevant to our context, then we may attempt a double experiment in the contemporary relevance of the ancient tradition.

First, then, we consider the interpretation that sees *the United States as carrier of "local tradition,"* by which I mean a "local tradition" of covenantal fidelity with strong and direct theological underpinnings. There is no doubt that such a theological underpinning is deep in U.S. self-understanding, as now exhibited in political discourse. The claim is not simply belated political pandering (though it is certainly that). The claim goes back all the way to the Puritan notion of "a city set on a hill," a theological vocation variously expressed as "Manifest Destiny," or currently as "leader of the free world." This brand of exceptionalism comes as close as is possible to understanding the United States as God's chosen people, a carrier of God's purpose amid a world of "godless nations."

But if that claim can be seriously entertained, then it is also the case that God's belatedly chosen people are also summoned to radical Torah obedience, to the living out of what is known of God's will for human society, a divine intention given currency with Martin Luther King, Jr.'s "I Have a Dream." The U.S. dream is a dream of "liberty and justice for all," though the justice component is most often subordinated in ideological rhetoric to the theme of liberty.

But the dream has not been tenaciously pursued. U.S. history has characteristically reshaped "chosenness" from Torah-based covenantalism to the ambitions of empire. The United States as a carrier of the "local tradition" stands under severe judgment for failure with the dream. In contemporary terms it is obvious enough to see that the United States is the primal perpetrator of global warming, which violates creation. (China, with a late start, might someday rival the United States as perpetrator, but not yet.) As the statistics make obvious, moreover, the United States is an unbearably violent society, both in terms of bodily violence and with reference to the economic violence that is intrinsic to our current economic arrangements. Add to these moral failures the savage history of racism in the United States, the primal "American Dilemma."[12] There is no need to detail these matters, even though prophetic imagination may continue to do so. It is enough to see that in terms of "local tradition," the United States stands under sharp indictment.

When the prophets indicted Israel in this way, they characteristically followed up with the "therefore" of prophetic sentence, that is, by the judgment and enactment of covenant curse. We can describe *indictment and sentence* in the "hot" terminology of religious conservatives. In this view God acts directly and immediately, as Jerry Falwell and others claimed with their portrayal of 9/11 as God's punishment for America's sins (though that list of "sins" was predictably and always committed by people other than religious conservatives). Or we can use the "cool" terminology that theological liberals prefer, claiming that "crimes against humanity" of various kinds and degrees breed their own "blowback" of punishment without direct divine agency. Thus we can imagine that exploitative policy will lead to social unrest, and that indifference to environment will lead to drought, storms, or other upheavals.[13] In either "hot" or "cool" rhetoric, the argument is an insistence that there is moral coherence to the creation guaranteed by the Creator, and even the special status as "chosen" does not exempt from consequences. This of course is a characteristic argument of the prophets against Israel.[14] If one pursues this way of interpretation, one might imagine that the United States, then, is under assault from empire (Islam? China?), which, at the behest of YHWH, works evil toward a failed chosen people.

But for reasons indicated in chapter 1, I find it more interesting and more compelling to see *the United States as empire* and not principally as carrier of local tradition. When the United States is taken as empire, it is easy enough to reread the prophetic tradition to which I have referred in order to suggest that the United States is cast as an imperial tool for YHWH in imposing sanctions upon wayward societies. As Assyria and Babylon were dispatched against a "godless nation" (Isaiah 10:6), so the United States might have been dispatched against a dictatorship that has savagely abused its own citizens. Of course such a reading was at the heart of the "crusade against communism" in the last century, in which the United States understood itself as the great savior of "lost" peoples.

But if that overlay from the prophets be accepted as usable grid and the United States as empire is understood with a divinely given vocation, then we must entertain as well the second step of prophetic imagination that we saw in Isaiah 10:7-14: the United States as empire oversteps its mandate, regards itself as free to act apart from God's purpose, and especially free to show no mercy toward those it opposes. If the United States is an empire in this way, then its failure to restrain itself from using atomic weapons, from using torture, and from killing civilians makes sense. The temptation to use shameless force afflicts all empires that are always trying to prove that violence in the empire's hands (and its hands alone!) is a good thing.

If it is to be faithful, the church in this nation must reckon with the ambiguous situation in which the United States is both *chosen people* and *empire*. Both readings together offer important ways that Scripture speaks to our contemporary context.

If we read the United States as chosen people, as *carrier of "local tradition,"* then the church must bring to the table a clearer, less compromised sense of what "chosenness" means. The church must insist that the public policy and public practice of the United States be measured against covenantal requirements of neighborly justice, mercy, and generosity. Such a society might be expected to organize its life and its resources around the shared destiny of haves and have-nots. For as far back as the tradition of Deuteronomy, the notion of "chosenness" had to do with attentiveness to needy neighbors. If the "year of remission" in Deuteronomy 15:1-18 is central to who Israel was as a chosen people, then even its own economy was subordinate to its obligation to its neighbors. Likewise today, the church's challenge is to summon civil society to its best self.[15]

On the other hand, it may be an easier case now to see *the United States as empire* that seeks to impose its will around the world, to demand "reform" as the price of engagement, and to monopolize resources in every possible way. As the prophets judge, such a superpower as Babylon is intrinsically unable to restrain itself, even as the acquisitive power of the United States is mostly beyond restraint. In such an environment God calls the church to carry the "local tradition," bearing witness against the empire's arrogance, greed, and insatiable appetites. It is likely that it comes only very late to every empire—including Babylon—to recognize itself as empire, to flex its muscles with restraint, to acknowledge the self-destructiveness of imagining autonomy that is not subject to any ordered morality or even to the community of nation-states. It may be the work of the church to name empire for what it is.

Here we are, then, in the twenty-first century, not unlike ancient Israel in the eighth or seventh century, waiting for Babylon. By the sixth century, Babylon had arrived, but hardly before. It was only in 605 BCE that Babylon was fully established after Assyria as the dominant power. And it was only in 598 that Babylon came into Jerusalem, a long time after prophetic anticipation. But the prophets knew long before that, just as poets always know long before the actual moment arrives. The poets speak only poetry, not program, not policy, not even advocacy, only poetry. But the poetry exists in order to make available what the ideologues are unable to see and what the policy makers are unable to grasp. By reminding their listeners of God's "therefore," the poets of Israel made their connections between today's acts of violation and tomorrow's inescapable outcomes, even as nearly everyone else thought themselves immune to that connection. The poets (then and now) dare connect the intransigence of heaven with the obtuseness of earth, and open a world of risk out beyond every settled formulation. The recovery of such poetic capacity is important in a community that cares about its local tradition. The task is not simply to reiterate old poetry, but to learn from its cadences what now needs to be uttered. Both *the distorted chosen people* and *the imperious empire* run roughshod over such utterance. But the poet never doubts that the utterance has staying power, for when rightly uttered, it may indeed be "a word from the LORD."

CHAPTER 3

THE LONG, SLOW PROCESS OF LOSS

Is it nothing to you, all you who pass by?
  Look and see
if there is any sorrow like my sorrow,
  which was brought upon me,
which the LORD inflicted
  on the day of his fierce anger. (Lamentations 1:12)

They have treated the wound of my people carelessly,
  saying, "Peace, peace,"
when there is no peace. (Jeremiah 6:14)

The loss of the city of Jerusalem, its temple and its king, was a loss that shattered the faith and identity of Jerusalem. The loss violated the deepest confidence and the most treasured assurances of the Jerusalem establishment. The new reality of public loss required deep and extended public grief that mourned and wept and chronicled the evaporation of viable life. The Book of Lamentations lines out the liturgical practice of grief.

But of course "official Jerusalem" had too much to lose, and so could not honestly participate in the grief. Rather, it had, as soon as possible, to set in motion a strategy of denial that tried to cover the loss and counter the grief. It is clear that official Jerusalem could dispatch establishment voices that moved public opinion beyond the reality of loss. Thus in ancient Jerusalem, as, for example, in the Book of Jeremiah, we may notice the interpretive contest between the voices of grief and the voices of denial that wanted to "move on."

In a parallel way, it is not difficult to see that the symbolism of 9/11 and the reality of economic collapse in the United States together are a harbinger of a dismantling of what seemed for a long time to be U.S. chosenness and exemption from the vulnerability of the world. The loss of the economic icon of the World Trade Center and damage to the military icon of the Pentagon bespeaks a deep symbolic loss that has soon been matched by the palpable loss of "normal" life in the United States as our public institutions are more or less in disarray. There is more than enough to grieve, and in church liturgy, folk music, and wistful comedy there continues to be honest grief. That honest grief, however, has most often been countered by official rhetoric that assures a return to normalcy, a recovery of the economy, and a continuation of security, well-being, and preeminence. It requires little imagination to see that our contemporary voicing of lamentations with its honest grief is countered by the denials that are set in motion as "business as usual." Indeed, the imperial apparatus seems to thrive on a mix of self-confidence and anxiety that wants no embrace of loss.

The "local tradition" of the Bible, for both Jews and Christians, knows all about loss. And empire, by its standard procedures and practices, requires local traditions to think about and process loss, because empire is always and everywhere depleting the life and energy of every local tradition.

The local tradition of the Bible, for Jews, knows loss deeply and perennially. The loss of Jerusalem at the hands of the Babylonians in the sixth century is the taproot of the loss tradition of Judaism. It is impossible to overstate the significance of the loss of Jerusalem for Jews. Consequently, on the ninth of the Jewish month of Av, faithful Jews continue to grieve the day when the Babylonian

Empire came and razed the temple, deported the king, and destroyed the city. Jews are not yet finished with that loss. And of course the long tale of loss for Jews has thus far culminated in the Shoah, the death of six million Jews that exposed the traditional faith as inadequate—or nearly inadequate—for the world of barbarity enacted in our time.[1]

Given the establishment power of Christianity in the West, the matter is of course very different for Christians. Yet at the heart of Christian faith, lying deep beneath its hegemonic institutional establishment, is the truth of loss for Christians, the crucifixion of Jesus.[2] To be sure, the "mystery of faith" regularly recited in the Christian Eucharist ("Christ has died, Christ is risen, Christ will come again") moves quickly beyond Friday loss to a new Easter beginning. But in fact it is the Friday death—the cross, the imperial execution—that Christians confess to be the ultimate disclosure of the power and love of God. While it is the case that Christians have not historically and culturally lived out—or had to live out—that defining loss, it is there. It lingers and it summons the faithful away from every triumphalism and every seduction of empire.

Thus Jews and Christians—very different from each other in social experience—are joined together in the intrusive awareness that at the center of truth is the durable force of historical loss. It is for that reason that Jews and Christians resort—Jews always, Christians in contemporary life—to the Book of Lamentations.[3]

In contrast to the "local tradition" of Jews and Christians, empires do not know about loss. Empires do not grieve, do not notice human suffering, do not acknowledge torn bodies or abused villages. Empires deal in quotas, statistics, summaries, and memos. And memos rarely mention loss; when they do, they disguise it in euphemism so that no one need notice. Empires characteristically do not notice loss because they are able to engage in reality-denying ideology that covers over everything in the splendor of power, victory, and stability. Empires do not acknowledge that many such claims are highly contested, and beyond contestation are frequently exhibited as false. But empires are undeterred by inconvenient truths, and rush on to persuasive certitude.

Thus I propose in this reflection on loss that we consider the tension between the *candor and acknowledgment* of the local tradition and the *capacity for denial* that characterizes empire. And when one lives, as Christian citizens in the United States do, between *local tradition and empire*, the contest between truth and pretense is an ongoing process that yields only provisional outcomes. If it is the case that "the truth makes free" (even truth about loss), then it is also true that "cover-up makes powerful." Our contemporary U.S. society is a contest between these claims.

The source of this ongoing process is the contest that was played out in ancient Jerusalem. The Jerusalem establishment had an enormous appetite for what we might call "hegemonic summary." Hegemonic summary celebrated, usually in liturgical setting, God's blessing of the monarchy of David and the temple of Solomon as a way to drown out the inconvenient fact of injustice in their midst. The great liturgical basis for the royal claims of the Davidic dynasty was the divine promise to David that assured the monarchy of YHWH's abiding, unconditional commitment: "I will not take my steadfast love from him, as I took it from Saul, whom I put away from before you. Your house and your kingdom shall be made sure forever before me; your throne shall be established forever" (2 Samuel 7:15-16).

The lyric Psalm 89, moreover, makes it clear that this initial divine oracle was reiterated on many liturgical occasions:

> Once and for all I have sworn by my holiness;
> I will not lie to David.
> His line shall continue forever,
> and his throne endure before me like the sun.
> It shall be established forever like the moon,
> an enduring witness in the skies. (vv. 35-37)

Claims for monarchy were matched by claims for the temple. Already in the founding liturgy of Solomon's newly dedicated temple, YHWH had promised to be a permanent resident in the temple and in the city: "The LORD has said that he would dwell in thick darkness. I have built you an exalted house, a place for you to dwell in forever" (1 Kings 8:12-13).

These two texts concerning dynasty and temple, regularly reiterated in state-sponsored liturgy, gave certitude and entitlement to those most closely gathered around the center of Jerusalem power.

All this certainty about God's blessing of Jerusalem, its king and its temple, gave the people of Jerusalem an excuse to ignore the social facts on the ground. If God was indeed blessing the power structure of Jerusalem unconditionally, then they need not worry about the economic exploitation and political oppression going on around them.

Arrayed against the formidable social power of this claim that God would never abandon Jerusalem was the relatively weak challenge of prophetic poetry. This ongoing but highly irregular tradition featured uncredentialed utterers with no social standing. Their sole authority came from (a) their imaginative, playful utterance; (b) their knowledge of the facts on the ground connected to human, bodily reality; and (c) the claim to be connected enough to speak the truth of YHWH.[4]

It turned out, of course, that these dissenting poets had it right. It turned out that the force of dynastic ideology and the high claims for the temple could not forestall imperial threat, a threat that the poets tied to covenantal tradition and to the disregard of the human neighborhood. Finally, belatedly, the long-awaited empire did arrive. In 598 BCE Babylon came and took away King Jehoiachin, the temple treasure, the officials, the artisans, the king's entourage, and just about everything else of value. It was a huge loss and it was an ending (2 Kings 24:10-16).

Enough remained, however (just barely), to allow those addicted to hegemonic summary to continue to fool themselves. There was a new king, Zedekiah, and life seemed to go on (2 Kings 24:17-18). That visible continuity, weak and vulnerable as it was, was enough to permit the faulty reliance on king and temple to persist, even in the face of harsh reality. Those enmeshed in that faulty urban ideology were permitted the short-term luxury of denial. They could pretend that the promises of YHWH would override the fierce reality of Babylon. They could imagine all of that because they had refused to understand the prophetic conviction: not only was Babylon an aggressive power; it was an instrument of YHWH's own intention for the city.

That denial, says Jeremiah—the poet closest to the crisis—permitted disregard of the facts on the ground:

> From the least to the greatest of them,
>   everyone is greedy for unjust gain;
> and from prophet to priest,
>   everyone deals falsely.
> They have treated the wound of my people carelessly,
>   saying, "Peace, peace,"
>   when there is no peace.
> They acted shamefully, they committed abomination;
>   yet they were not ashamed,
>   they did not know how to blush.
> Therefore they shall fall among those who fall;
>   at the time that I punish them,
>   they shall be overthrown, says the LORD.
>   (Jeremiah 6:13-15)

The well-known mantra "shalom, shalom" is immediately countered by the poetic insistence "There is no shalom." Saying "peace" does not create peace. The poet echoes the official claim and then refutes it. This terse interaction of officialdom and its refutation is preceded in verse 13 by an indictment of the phoniness of official business and official leadership. And it is followed in verse 15 with the labeling of official Jerusalem as "abomination," followed by the "therefore" of prophetic anticipation of the "stumbling" to come. And then the whole of this truth-telling utterance is reiterated in the tradition yet again in 8:10-12. The poet describes the denial of official Jerusalem. The establishment is well practiced in denial, because the liturgical mantra has covered over the failures of policy.

The drama of denial and exposure is made specific in the narrative account of Jeremiah 27–28, wherein Jeremiah meets Hananiah, a powerful advocate for establishment faith. The "yoke" of 27:2 signifies the imperial hegemony that Babylon is about to impose on Jerusalem. The imposition is to be accomplished by "King Nebuchadnezzar of Babylon, my servant" (27:6). But this truth-telling about failed Jerusalem is challenged by Hananiah:

> Thus says the LORD of hosts, the God of Israel: I have broken the yoke of the king of Babylon. Within two years I will bring back to this place all the vessels of the LORD's house, which King Nebuchadnezzar of Babylon took away from this place and carried to Babylon. I will also bring back to this place King Jeconiah son of Jehoiakim of Judah, and all the exiles from Judah who went to Babylon, says the LORD, for I will break the yoke of the king of Babylon. (28:2-4)

The narrative continues. It presents a contest between an ideology of certitude and the raw poetry of contradiction. Hananiah did not invent his insistence. He is a child and product of Jerusalem exceptionalism. He is schooled in the tradition of Isaiah, who, a century earlier, had declared Jerusalem immune to imperial threat (Isaiah 37:33-35). Hananiah only echoes that certitude. But what he did not understand, as his sponsors did not understand, is that the old tradition could no longer be relied upon against a God-dispatched empire now on a mission of disruption.

The official mantra could not hold. The denial could not be sustained. The uncredentialed poetry turned out to be the truth. Babylon did come. A yoke of empire was imposed. The empire ran roughshod over the city. Yet the tradition of Jeremiah did not grant absolute authority and power to the empire, because it always remembered that empires are transitory and provisional. Thus, in the very text concerning Hananiah, the Jeremiah tradition carefully and defiantly said, "until":

> All the nations shall serve him and his son and his grandson, *until* the time of his own land comes; then many nations and great kings shall make him their slave. (27:7, emphasis added)

> I will punish that nation with the sword, with famine, and with pestilence, says the LORD, *until* I have completed its destruction by his hand. (27:8, emphasis added)

> They shall be carried to Babylon, and there they shall stay, *until* the day when I give attention to them, says the LORD. Then I will bring them up and restore them to this place. (27:22, emphasis added)

There is an "until" still to come, but not soon. In this dramatic moment the poetry of truth-telling breaks the spell of the old ideologies of the city.

Eventually there will be hope. Eventually there will be—in the mid-sixth century—an explosion of new literature voicing YHWH's new promises. All of that will come, eventually. But just now our question is about the interim, the meantime of foreseeable future with nothing new on the horizon, the time that the tradition inscrutably calls "seventy years."[5] Well, for that interim, for however long it will be, there is empire. There is Babylon. There is deportation. There is loss. There is a pause in triumphalist ideology. And there is also, before there could be new hope, abiding local tradition carried by the poets. That local tradition, now in a time of loss, became the habitat for grief. The loss created space for and evoked the Book of Lamentations, the practice of grief, the capacity for truth-telling about loss. This poetry of grief directly contradicts the old ideology of Jerusalem. More than that, it is a tearful defiance thrown in the face of empire. The weepers in their weeping said, "We will not be silent. We will not swallow our tears.

We will tell the truth about loss. We cannot do more than that. But for now we do not need to do more than that."

The Book of Lamentations invites us to imagine a long pause in both certitude and denial. It is a long pause against old temptations and against new imperial impingement. The pause is in order to honor and cherish and valorize this powerful moment of undoing. No need to rush, as there is nowhere to rush to. Linger. Linger in the ashes and tears, and ponder the truth that makes one free. In that moment of Lamentations, the sixth-century weepers reenacted the old voice of their ancestors: "After a long time the king of Egypt died. The Israelites groaned under their slavery, and cried out" (Exodus 2:23).

Like their ancestors, they did not know if the grief would be heard. Heard or not, it must be uttered fully, honestly, unprotected by ideology, unintimidated by empire, the full honoring of the grief of the body, raw, complete, crafted, available, putting all old certitudes to risk.

The five chapters of the Book of Lamentations contain five poems of grief, four of which are acrostic, running from A to Z in an attempt to voice the fullness of grief and loss. There is nothing here of denial. There is nothing here of appeal to the old certitudes of king or temple. There is only the raw failure and emptiness of the moment given artistic articulation. The first poem begins with acknowledgment of the reversal of the city:

> How lonely sits the city
>   that once was full of people!
> How like a widow she has become,
>   she that was great among the nations!
> She that was a princess among the provinces
>   has become a vassal. (Lamentations 1:1)

The contrast between then and now, offered in parallels of contrast, is without reserve:

lonely . . . full;
widow . . . great;
princess . . . vassal.[6]

The city now is in the grip of empire. And the local tradition, in its candor, can only be truthful about loss and grief. The city has no one to comfort (1:2, 9, 17, 21). At the outset poems 1 and 2 are simply voices of pain that tilt over to accusation against God. Later on in the Book of Lamentations, there will be attempts to find meaning in the loss. But not yet. Here there is no attempt at rationalization. Here all sense-making is deferred.[7] For the moment the candor of Israel in loss is enough to evoke accusation against YHWH for having abandoned or abused the children:

Look, O Lord, and consider!
    To whom have you done this?
Should women eat their offspring,
    the children they have borne? (Lamentations 2:20)

As we move through the poems, we are able to see the move beyond raw pain to understanding, but the understanding that comes cannot come too soon, or else it becomes denial. In the latter part of the poetry of Lamentations,

- there is confession of sin, entertaining the thought that the destruction is merited punishment (3:42);
- there is remembrance of ancient divine fidelity (3:21-24);
- there is memory of a divine utterance of "fear not" that transformed (3:57), but as Linafelt observes, "There is never an indication . . . that such a 'fear not' is on the present horizon."[8]

The attempt at rationalization does not prevail. In the midst of such remembrance and acknowledgment, there is still a strong sense of meaningless in the loss:

> Those who were my enemies without cause
>   have hunted me like a bird;
> they flung me alive into a pit
>   and hurled stones on me;
> water closed over my head;
>   I said, "I am lost." (3:52-54)

The central claim is clear: "I am lost" (3:54).[9] In due course (whenever that may be), Israel's poetry will move on. But first, it is candid about loss, aware of pain without explanation, refusing guilt, in doubting wonderment about YHWH. The local tradition goes to the bottom of known reality, way beneath ideology, summary, or meaning. The comforts of empire are seen to be no comfort at all, neither the old way of establishment Jerusalem nor the new way of Babylon can offer solace.

Now practitioners of this local tradition in the United States practice faith yet again in the midst of empire. The U.S. empire, since the fall of the Soviet Union in 1989, is beyond challenge.[10] As a consequence, it has become bold about imposing its will everywhere that it can; it is a will imposed militarily, a will imposed economically through the required "reforms" of the World Bank and the IMF, a will imposed by an arbitrary refusal to participate in treaties or accept application of the rule of law to agents of the empire.

But then, in the midst of a waxing empire that was the beneficiary of "the end of history," came 9/11.[11] In one way of assessment, 9/11 was a fairly modest event with a relatively small number of deaths. However, the symbolic significance of the event has grossly outweighed its "factual" reality. That disjunction results partly from the fact that 9/11 occurred in the center of media attention in New York and Washington, partly because it was aimed at the core power icon and the core money icon of our society, and partly because it happened "on our shores."

The shock and anxious fear evoked by 9/11 are deep and acute, because it unmasked an abiding delusion of American life: that we are somehow exempt from the vulnerability that defines life for the rest of the world. The ideological assumption of U.S. exceptionalism—not unlike the Davidic-temple claims of the Old Testament—assumed and assured a privileged, entitled future. It was a future guaranteed by military monopoly and economic preeminence, but such monopoly and preeminence are in the service of an implicit theological claim of "goodness" and "chosenness."[12] And all of that was enacted with gestures of profound disrespect and savage hostility toward much of the rest of the world. Beyond the loss of lives (that itself is not to be unappreciated), there was, in 9/11, a loss of innocence about which Niebuhr wrote so relentlessly: the loss of certitude, the loss of entitlement, and the fresh recognition of vulnerability.

So how to respond to this disaster that has now been followed by an unraveling of the social infrastructure evoked by a failure to notice and limit greed? Predictably, the empire denied. The script of the empire might have been written by Hananiah. It featured a brief liturgical acknowledgment by the president in the National Cathedral, and then immediately, without any critical self-reflection, on to recovery; aggressive, bombastic platitudes culminating in "Bring it on," a bullying formula for invincibility. I judge that this conduct was not simply the peculiar performance of the unknowing president (though it was that), but that he had caught the flavor of the body politic in its uninterrupted will to hegemony. The empire did not linger over loss. It did not attend to the slow, steady voices of pain, choosing even to keep invisible the returning body bags from Iraq and Afghanistan. It did not entertain the thought that U.S. policy and conduct might be responsible for provoking the attack. It did not compute the profound contradiction between the claim of "leader of the free world" and the rapacious occupation of the world for the sake of markets, resources, and control. The empire doesn't question itself; it "sucks it up" and moves on, restoring its hegemony and bringing the dissenters to justice.

This denial tried to paper over the profound anxiety that the posturing of the Department of Homeland Security has brought about. But the empire really doesn't want that anxiety to go away, because it creates the hostility and rage that feed imperial ideology. By pandering to and co-opting anxiety among its citizens, the empire creates the "need" for even tighter hegemony, and at the same time devours any who try to resist its passion for control.

In the midst of the "surge" of empire that regards itself as capable of anything and entitled to everything, sits the local tradition of Jews and Christians, with its unyielding texts that testify to another way. This local tradition, which stands in deep tension with the empire, knows that denial cannot finally cover over the reality of loss and grief. It knows that the anxiety must be given full-bodied expression, and that the forces of control and acquisitiveness must be silent when confronted by it. When it can, empire tries to co-opt loss, making it a quick and easy means to wring fresh loyalty and resentment of outsiders from its citizens. Thus we witness the theft of the local tradition in the service of the empire.

But the local tradition knows that there is no quick fix for loss; there is no easy resolve of anxiety; there is no ready antidote to widely felt vulnerability. The congregation of the local tradition, having inhaled so much imperial air, is itself slow and reluctant to realize what has been entrusted to it in these poems of candor. Such a congregation is tempted to collude with and accommodate itself to the loud, insistent practices of the empire. At its best, however, the congregation, funded by local tradition, knows better.

As a consequence, I believe as a direct consequence of the durable faith of the congregation, we are now beneficiaries of a whole new wave of scholarship on laments in general and about the Book of Lamentations in particular. Of course the connections between the felt need of a particular communal culture and the directions of scholarship are never made explicit, and are mostly not acknowledged by scholars themselves. I believe nonetheless that critical study is led by the hungers of its constituency. It is as though a large body of scholars has implicitly understood that ours is now a culture of faith that must find resources for elemental human reality that refuses the cover-up of empire. This resolve to mobilize such resources is evident in both more critical and more pastoral enterprises.

In critical scholarship, we have a steady flow of new commentaries on the Book of Lamentations, notably by Adele Berlin, John Bracke, F. W. Dobbs-Allsopp, Erhard Gerstenberger, and Kathleen O'Connor, all since the turn of the century.[13] I understand, of course, that some of this is just a need to "complete the series," so that in any commentary series there must, perforce, be one on Lamentations. But if one contrasts this work with earlier acts of "completing the series," one can see a new gravitas and contemporaneity even in the production of formal commentaries. Alongside the commentaries, moreover, are a number of quite remarkable studies of which I note the following:

- Scott Ellington, *Risking Truth*, carries the issue of lament into the New Testament;[14]
- Nancy Lee, *The Singers of Lamentations*, links the Book of Lamentations to the contemporary poetry of suffering and hope that has come out of the violence of the Serbian, Croatian, Bosnia conflict;[15]
- Tod Linafelt, *Surviving Lamentations*, has considered the way in which Lamentations is a "literature of survival" in the Jewish tradition that he carries into present-day violence and hope in Judaism;[16]
- Carleen Mandolfo, D*aughter Zion Talks Back to the Prophets*, finds the dialogic form of the Book of Lamentations to be both a means to resist the alien work of God so championed by the prophets as well as a voice of hope in God.[17]
- Kathleen O'Connor, *Lamentations & the Tears of the World*, has extended her commentary, as the title of her book indicates, toward present-day suffering, violence, and despair.[18]

46

She has understood that in the contemporary world, as in the ancient world, candor is a prerequisite to comfort, and protest is a way back to the goodness of God.

As I write this, I have just received a copy of a new volume of essays on lament edited by Nancy Lee and Carleen Mandolfo, *Lamentations in Ancient and Contemporary Cultural Contexts*.[19] This remarkable collection has a number of important critical essays, but then offers commentary on contemporary lament in China, among African American women, in Croatia, in Iraq, in South Africa, in New Orleans, and among victims of HIV and AIDS. This sampling makes available the woundedness of the world that refuses to be silenced by any hegemonic power, political, economic, military, or ecclesial. While these contemporary laments are the product of contemporary courage and candor, there can be no doubt that they are rooted in this ancient text of truth-telling. There would be sad and high irony if it turned out that the only venue in the world that was unable or unwilling to engage in such rhetoric at the throne would be the culture of the establishment West, so schooled in Enlightenment consciousness, that has most studied the text scientifically but has kept it remote from the artistic, liturgical, pastoral life of the people. The contrast between the testimony of these other cultures cited in these discussions and the propensity of the empire is astounding and summoning.

Along with such critical study, we also have a growing literature of a more pastoral tone concerning the laments. Among those known to me are the following, in the order of publication:

- Kathleen Billman and Daniel Migliore, *Rachel's Cry*;[20]
- Michael Jinkins, *In the House of the Lord*;[21]
- Stephen P. McCutchan, *Experiencing the Psalms*;[22]
- Michael Card, *A Sacred Sorrow*;[23]
- Patrick D. Miller and Sally A. Brown, *Lament*;[24]
- Kristin M. Swenson, *Living Through Pain*.[25]

And I mention four more derivative studies: Ann Weems, *Psalms of Lament* (1995), on the death of her beloved Todd; John O'Brien, *Cry Me a River* (2008), ruminations of a Roman Catholic monk on the woundedness of the church; *Poets on the Psalms*, edited by Lynn Domina (2008), an elegant statement from contemporary poets on the artistry and religious power of the Psalms; and Wesley Stevens, *Learning to Sing in a Strange Land*, a report on how the Psalms mattered decisively when his daughter was imprisoned.[26]

Taken as a whole, a flood of literature has emerged that is deeply in touch with human reality that must be rendered according to the ancient cadences of pain and possibility. If we ask why this explosion of literature, we cannot credit it simply to a scholarly interest or a need to "cover" this part of the canon. I have no doubt that this literature is offered to us because of a widespread, deeply known awareness that the imperial culture in which we live has failed in human vocation, and there is need to line out in daring ways the acute vulnerability out of which social, cultural newness may arise.

Of course much hard work remains for the transposition of this fresh awareness into more generally available form that may heal and restore the public imagination of our society.[27] Such reengagement with the elemental cries of faith is urgent among us because such a cry of protest, indignation, and insistence embodies a resolve to depart the easy demands of hegemony and to practice in truthfulness the bodily life of the world, the kind of scarred, wounded bodily life that the empire refuses. This opportunity to recover the practice of lament is part of a contest . . . whether the empire can silence or whether the local tradition will have its say, whether human possibilities will be reduced to control and conformity, or whether the juices of newness can be channeled through shrill voice and urgent tears. Caught as we are between empire and local tradition, one might imagine God's suffering spirit asking,

Is it nothing to you, all you who pass by?
Look and see
if there is any sorrow like my sorrow. (Lamentations 1:12)

Is it nothing to you?
Do you notice?
Will you pause?
Will you join the vulnerability?
Our response does not come easily, schooled as we are in imperial denial.

CHAPTER 4

THE DIVINE AS THE POETIC

Surely I know the plans I have for you, says the LORD, plans
for your welfare and not for harm, to give you a future with
hope. Then when you call upon me and come and pray to
me, I will hear you. When you search for me, you will find
me; if you seek me with all your heart, I will let you find me,
says the LORD, and I will restore your fortunes and gather
you from all the nations and all the places where I have
driven you, says the LORD, and I will bring you back to the
place from which I sent you into exile. (Jeremiah 29:11-14)

The displacement of leading members of Jerusalem society to
Babylon might have ended in despair. There was ample reason to
conclude that YHWH's promises were exhausted and hope was
spent: "So I say, 'Gone is my glory, and all that I had hoped for
from the LORD' " (Lamentations 3:18).

That, however, is not what happened. In the very midst of
such a seemingly hopeless situation, new hope was voiced. New
promises were uttered. New poems were offered that alleged to
be YHWH's very own commitment to the future of Jerusalem
and its erstwhile inhabitants. Thus the divine resolve to bring
the deportees home came to be a vigorous assertion and shaping
conviction within the exilic community. No reason is given for

such a hope, except that it was taken to be grounded in YHWH's own resolve.

In contemporary United States culture, it is not yet clear how such an emergence of hope might occur. It is certain that the old, tired imperial ideology to which much corporate wealth and much military power is committed cannot yield such possibility. Mostly in the midst of societal disarray what we get is moralistic or ideological posturing. Neither of these can amount to a possible newness outside the categories of what is old and failed. There are, to be sure, voices of hope. None of these are more powerful or compelling than the "I Have a Dream" of Martin Luther King, Jr. But such "dreaming" must perforce be grounded well beyond business as usual, and it is only the "local tradition" of faith that dares to speak in this way. Perhaps it is the case that a hope-filled future for our society depends upon the courage and freedom of the local tradition to speak beyond accepted categories for the sake of grace-filled newness. There is a "plan," perhaps, beyond our conventional possibilities. That "plan," however, requires "seeking with all your heart." Such a practice in a weary culture will at best be odd. But its oddness does not make it impossible.

In the sixth century, Jews, as displaced persons, lived with and under the pressure of Babylon. Some lived in Babylon and some were scattered elsewhere; many continued to live in the homeland. But all were to some extent displaced by the imposing insistent power of the empire.

In this season of displacement, we do not know what all the Jews did, though we know that they were admonished to settle in, to build houses, to plant gardens, and to marry off their young (Jeremiah 29:5-6). No doubt they went about their economic business, coming to terms with Babylonian reality in a variety of ways. But we also know, as indicated in the previous chapter, that they grieved over what had been lost:

By the rivers of Babylon—
there we sat down and there we wept
when we remembered Zion. (Psalm 137:1)

And they continued well into the next century to grieve over what had been lost:

They replied, "The survivors there in the province who escaped captivity are in great trouble and shame; the wall of Jerusalem is broken down, and its gates have been destroyed by fire." When I heard these words I sat down and wept, and mourned for days, fasting and praying before the God of heaven. (Nehemiah 1:3-4)

They cried out in their need, even as their ancient ancestors had "cried out" in their distress (Exodus 2:23). Their crying had been framed by the resilient memory they had of poetry they had heard. It was *unwelcome poetry* that they remembered, poetry from Amos and Micah and Isaiah and Jeremiah, lining out in anticipation the loss and devastation to come. That poetry had preceded the empire. That poetry had spoken of the empire only incidentally, because its true subject was YHWH, who uttered words of disappointment concerning Israel and consequently words of threat. The season of disappointment gave the displaced a long time to remember and to ponder that poetry of anticipated loss. The sense of displacement gave time to collect and order such poetry into coherent patterns that were on the way to canon. But mostly they listened—again and again—to the cadences of divine disappointment and alienation that sounded a steady beat of loss. The poetry was old; but its effect was to create a contemporary context for lament. The lamentation was the *human response of Israel to the divine poetry of alienation*. The poetry was true, it turned out, and so the grief was loud and deep.

The local tradition of the *poetry of alienation* and *response in grief* is so characteristically Jewish. It yields the prophetic and the liturgical voice of the sixth-century crisis of abandonment. It is a quite distinctive and treasured local tradition that shaped lived reality in a particular way. To appreciate fully that local tradition of prophetic poetry and liturgical response, we should contrast it with the empire's own liturgy. The empire's liturgy was all doxology, all praise, all celebration, all self-affirmation, and all victorious confidence. The empire had no room for sadness, loss, or grief. Unwelcome poetry never found voice in the empire, for the poets of unwelcome were all silenced. The empire permitted no cry, expected no response, engaged in no dialogue, offered no ultimate holiness . . . and so practiced an unrecognized despair and an uninterrupted denial.

One can imagine, then, two parallel liturgies. On the one hand, the imperial liturgy was about unthinking affirmation. On the other hand, Jewish local tradition's practice hosted unwelcome poems and unsilenced cries of need as a response to real or anticipated loss. The issue for displaced Jews is whether they could sustain the theological tradition about which they sat down and wept. In the local tradition the ultimate reality of God and the immediate reality of loss grappled with each other. "But," the Jews asked themselves, "should we abandon the local tradition in order to settle down to life in the empire?" That, of course, is always the question for this (and any other) local tradition: whether to relinquish or retain, whether to accommodate or resist, whether to give one's self over to hegemony's buoyant self-delusions or to live in contradiction to that buoyancy. It was an acute question for those displaced Jews, even as now the same question faces the church in the midst of empire. The question never receives a final or a simple answer. The issue is always under negotiation and review; the local tradition is always repositioning itself and, at the same time, always being imposed upon by the force of the empire. So it must have been among Jews in Babylon, hearing always again the refrain of the unwelcome poetry of divine disappointment, always again responding in grief, always again refusing to give up on that ancient rootage.

And there, in the midst of the "always again," there came a new poetry that bears all the mark of *welcome*. It is, in this case, an inexplicable wonder that the community of local tradition that keeps hearing the old poetry of unwelcome is gifted by new poetry that sounds in a fresh cadence. It is a wonder beyond explanation. Sooner or later the empire might have caused the poetry of the local tradition to evaporate—but it did not happen that way. Rather, all the coercive force of empire is said to become the seedbed and venue for new poetry that was heard among Jews as a voice, and therefore as the presence, of God, the God who has refused to abandon the displaced. It may be that the new poetry of welcome,

- is to be understood as raw human hope that in resilience just would not give in;
- is to be understood as evidence of the ideological force of those who dominated sixth-century Jewish imagination, who imposed the notion of "return and restoration" on a community that would otherwise have settled for a new home in empire;
- is finally to be taken as the gift of YHWH's own resolve for the future that stands against the facts on the ground.

Whether raw human hope, or ideologically led, or divinely appointed—or all of the above—the new poetry of welcome becomes the ground for a fresh future. Surely it would not have happened to a community that had quit on its own imaginative discourse for the sake of the flat, one-dimensional, coercive prose of the empire. That new poetry—however it is generated—reached some with open ears, precisely the ones who had groaned most candidly. Presumably the poetry could not have reached those who had given up on rootage and who freely and willingly adapted to a new imperial reality. The local tradition culminates in a readiness for a time of new poetry. And when it is uttered, it is heard as a forceful assurance that exile is the habitat of the holy, and that the empire has not been able—for all its effort—to eliminate YHWH as the definitive player in the shape of the future.

Thus we may ponder what it is like for the children of the local tradition to hear poetry of welcome amid the prosaic control of the empire. This poetry moves boldly in images and metaphors out beyond the imperial world. It takes up old treasured, trusted themes and voices them in contemporary idiom.[1] It dares to suggest that another reality exists beyond the empire's control. It invites new social possibility. It mocks the empire that they had come to trust and fear too much. And it does so because at the center of this poetry, the alleged speaker of new possibility is none other than YHWH, whom the empire could neither silence nor domesticate. Simply by being spoken and heard, the poetry creates a new social freedom. It imagines otherwise; it invites its listeners to walk boldly into the world it creates. It authorizes courage, summons defiance, and lines out resistance, all in the interest of legitimating the compelling force of the local tradition.

As we are able to imagine what it was like to hear such poetry, so we may wonder what it is like to utter it. Taken humanly, the voices we can identify must have been seized by a restless passion that surged against their own prudence.[2] But I refer not to the human utterer, but rather to the divine utterer of this poetry. For this rhetoric is from none other than the lips of YHWH! It is in the character of YHWH to give voice to poetic cadence. Poetic form is indispensable for speech that matches YHWH's own restless freedom.[3] Sometimes, to be sure, the tradition exhibits YHWH slowed to memo and rule and syllogism—but not mostly.[4] Mostly YHWH, in poetic utterance, authorizes candor and sounds grief and issues hope that opens to new possibility. In the prophetic poetry YHWH seeks to penetrate the fearful anxiety of Israel, to energize by defying the given and disturbing the presumed world in which the listeners lived. YHWH knows, always knows, that the empire is penultimate; its time will pass.[5] YHWH's words anticipate a future for Israel beyond the empire. As a consequence, Jewish life in

Babylon, local tradition in empire, is voiced in revelatory, defiant, anticipatory terms that the empire can neither silence nor contain. In what follows I will consider in turn (a) the three great poetic voices of exile, (b) the political connections of these voices of poetry, and (c) narrative counterpoints to the three bearers of poetry. The sum of this analysis will be concerned with the canon; fixed through exilic poetic daring, it provides steady ground for local tradition against every confiscation or reductionism.

A. THREE WAVES OF POETRY

1. Ezekiel

The prophet Ezekiel, for the most part, does not write poetry. His work, however, is powerfully imaginative and in any case moves well beyond conventional prose. I take his visionary work as poetry because he invites his listeners—readers—to entertain a world of possibility out beyond "the given." As he has "imagined" the destruction of Jerusalem, so he takes the lead, among the displaced, in imagining a future. Here I will comment on a series of representative texts that exhibit the art of "listening to poetry" as a way of survival amid Babylonian pressure.

First, the poet Ezekiel delivers poetic scenarios toward those who have been the great adversaries of Jerusalem. Of Tyre (who wished Jerusalem ill) he writes,

> See, I am against You, O Tyre!
>   I will hurl many nations against you,
>   as the sea hurls its waves.
> They shall destroy the walls of Tyre
>   and break down its towers.
> I will scrape its soil from it
>   and make it a bare rock.
> It shall become, in the midst of the sea,

a place for spreading nets.
I have spoken, says the Lord GOD.
It shall become plunder for the nations,
  and its daughter-towns in the country
  shall be killed by the sword.
Then they shall know that I am the LORD.
          (Ezekiel 26:3-6; see 28:6-10)

In the poem YHWH takes active initiative to exercise sovereignty over the geopolitical scene. It is, moreover, not different concerning Egypt, that constant vexation to the city:

I am against you, Pharaoh king of Egypt,
the great dragon sprawling in the midst of its channels,
saying, "My Nile is my own; I made it for myself."
I will put hooks in your jaws,
  and make the fish of your channels stick to your scales.
I will draw you up from your channels,
  with all the fish of your channels
  sticking to your scales.
I will fling you into the wilderness,
  you and all the fish of your channels;
you shall fall in the open field,
  and not be gathered and buried.
To the animals of the earth and to the birds of the air
  I have given you as food.
Then all the inhabitants of Egypt shall know
  that I am the LORD
because you were a staff of reed to the house of Israel;
when they grasped you with the hand, you broke,
  and tore all their shoulders;
and when they leaned on you, you broke,
  and made all their legs unsteady. (Ezekiel 29:3-7)

These poems of Ezekiel vigorously assert YHWH's sovereignty and intentionality:

Then they shall know that I am [YHWH]. (26:6)
For I have spoken, says the Lord GOD. (28:10)

> Then all the inhabitants of Egypt shall know that I am
> the LORD. (29:6)

The intent and effect of the poetry is to wrest sovereignty from the powers that had intimidated and abused Israel.

Scholars have regularly noticed that Ezekiel, unlike Isaiah and Jeremiah, offers no oracle directly against Babylon.[6] That fact is perhaps an indication that even poets must pay some attention to political reality.[7] These oracles, moreover, do not say anything about the future of displaced Israel. But much is implied. Any listener could readily infer that the elimination of adversaries creates breathing space for the community gathered around the poet.

Some passages in Ezekiel, however, do articulate an anticipated well-being for the displaced community. In 34:11-16, for example, Ezekiel presents YHWH as the protective God of Israel who willingly and directly accepts governance of the community that had suffered because of bad shepherds (king). Now the poor leadership that caused displacement is displaced by YHWH's direct rule:

> I myself will search for my sheep, and will seek them out.
> . . . I myself will be the shepherd of my sheep, and I will make
> them lie down, says the Lord GOD. I will seek the lost, and I
> will bring back the strayed, and I will bind up the injured, and
> I will strengthen the weak, but the fat and the strong I will
> destroy. I will feed them with justice. (34:11, 15-16)

The new shepherd will create a milieu of shalom that will be a sharp alternative to present circumstance. That act will cause a renovation of creation as well as a historical restoration:

> I will make with them a covenant of peace and banish wild
> animals from the land, so that they may live in the wild and
> sleep in the woods securely. I will make them and the region
> around my hill a blessing; and I will send down the showers
> in their season; they shall be showers of blessing. The trees of
> the field shall yield their fruit, and the earth shall yield its
> increase. They shall be secure on their soil; and they shall

know that I am the LORD, when I break the bars of their yoke, and save them from the hands of those who enslaved them. (34:25-27)

So speaks a poet who does not need to explain or comment on "secondary causes," the means YHWH will employ to accomplish this restoration. It is enough to imagine, for such imagining authorizes and empowers and invites initiative-taking.[8]

The rhetoric of restoration abounds in this poetry. In 36:24-29, the poet can tersely embrace motifs of homecoming (v. 24), cultic cleansing to qualify to be in YHWH's presence (v. 25), a new will for obedience (v. 26), and a revivification of the fruitfulness of creation (v. 29). The poetry is clearly designed to shake the displaced out of lethargy, despair, and excessive accommodation to the force of empire.

The imagery of homecoming is even more direct in 37:1-14, wherein homecoming is likened to the resurrection of the dead: "I am going to open your graves, and bring you up from your graves, O my people; and I will bring you back to the land of Israel" (v. 12).[9]

This imagery fully acknowledges the depth of death to which the displaced have sunk. But that depth is powerfully countered by the soaring possibility whereby, " 'You shall know that I, the LORD, have spoken and will act,' says the LORD" (v. 14).

The divine resolve renews the covenant that Israel's disobedience had placed in such jeopardy: "I will make a covenant of peace with them; it shall be an everlasting covenant with them; and I will bless them and multiply them, and will set my sanctuary among them forevermore" (37:26).

Two terms for covenant, *peace* and *everlasting*, are used, and the verse ends in renewal creation and assurance of divine presence. The poet counters the dismal status of exiles by an eloquent scenario of new beginning.

The motif of divine presence sounded in 37:26 is fleshed out in the final vision of temple presence (chaps. 40–48). The glory of YHWH that had departed the city in chapter 10 now returns in power and splendor:

> The glory of the God of Israel was coming from the east; the sound was like the sound of mighty waters, and the earth shone with his glory. The vision I saw was like the vision that I had seen when he came to destroy the city, and like the vision that I had seen by the river Chebar; and I fell upon my face. As the glory of the LORD entered the temple by the gate facing east, the spirit lifted me up, and brought me into the inner court; and the glory of the LORD filled the temple (43:2-5).

The glory that had seemed tentative and provisional is now "forever" (vv. 7, 9). It is no wonder that finally the new name of the city, imagined by the poet, is "The LORD is There" (48:35).

The prophet speaks these words in direct contradiction to the facts on the ground. It is the work of poets to contradict the facts on the ground and to invite the listeners to embrace an alternative future. The poetry is grounded in a deep theological memory. But finally it depends on (inspired?) imagination to summon the community to an alternative reality. In all of these texts, poetic, imaginative discourse is required to circumvent the hopelessness of Babylonian reality. No one could see how to get from here to there. But the poet is into vision, not explanation. Those visions, moreover, are heard among the displaced as God's own committed utterance that alters the templates of historical circumstance.

2. Jeremiah

Jeremiah, like Ezekiel, had offered his share of "unwelcome poetry," utilizing various images of infidelity, terminal illness, and war in order to show YHWH's attitude toward Jerusalem. Like Ezekiel, the Jeremiah tradition eventually turns from unwelcome to "welcome poetry," the latter an invitation to trust and imagine and act beyond the devastation and displacement. While Jeremiah is a contemporary of Ezekiel, his poetic imagery moves in a quite different direction concerning covenant and land. Whereas Ezekiel is preoccupied with the uncompromising holiness of YHWH, Jeremiah focuses on the wounded, betrayed fidelity of YHWH. Jeremiah's more lyrical poetry penetrates down to the very bottom of faith issues. Jeremiah's poetry of new possibility occurs largely in chapters 29–33, and seeks to function, as does the promissory material of Ezekiel, to shake the displaced out of their deep despair and capitulation to imperial definitions of reality.[10] Out of this rich poetry, I will mention only four texts.

In 30:12-17 the poet takes up the imagery of terminal illness from 8:22.[11] Verses 12-15 accent the deep and hopeless situation of failed Israel, now without allies or agents of healing. But then, in a stunning rhetorical maneuver, the poem has YHWH reverse field. The same voice that declared, "Your hurt is incurable" (v. 12), now asserts:

> I will restore health to you,
>   and your wounds I will heal, says the LORD,
> because they have called you an outcast:
>   "It is Zion; no one cares for her!" (v. 17)

The about-face of the poem reflects the remarkable about-face of YHWH, who utters the poem that eventuates in an about-face for Israel's historical destiny. The incurable will be healed!

A second image concerns the "scattered" (displaced) who will be "gathered" (brought home). Jeremiah imagines a great procession of "scattered" Israelites being brought home by YHWH:

> See, I am going to bring them from the land of the north,
>   and gather them from the farthest parts of the earth,
> among them the blind and the lame,
>   those with child and those in labor, together;
>   a great company, they shall return here.
> With weeping they shall come,
>   and with consolations I will lead them back,

I will let them walk by brooks of water,
  in a straight path in which they shall not stumble;
for I have become a father to Israel,
  and Ephraim is my firstborn. (31:8-9)

And in the next verse the two terms of the news—scattered, gathered—are placed in close parallel so that the reversal cannot be missed:

Hear the word of the LORD, O nations,
  and declare it in the coastlands far away;
say, "He who scattered Israel will gather him,
  and will keep him as a shepherd a flock." (31:10)

Better known is Jeremiah's promissory oracle concerning the new (or better, "renewed") covenant. The old one has been broken in disobedience, but YHWH, as in Exodus 34:9-10, is willing to begin again with Israel. The new relation of YHWH with Israel will again be concerned with Torah obedience (v. 33) and will be made possible by YHWH's willingness to forgive (v. 34):

This is the covenant that I will make with the house of Israel after those days, says the LORD: I will put my law within them, and I will write it on their hearts; and I will be their God, and they shall be my people. No longer shall they teach one another, or say to each other, "Know the LORD," for they shall all know me, from the least of them to the greatest, says the LORD; for I will forgive their iniquity, and remember their sin no more. (31:33-34)

The renewal is from the side of YHWH; YHWH's profound fidelity will have a transformative impact on Israel, who will no longer be wayward.

In chapter 32 Jeremiah buys a piece of land from his cousin. This simple transaction between two family members, however, points toward a much broader assurance that those who have been displaced will one day secure their land:

Thus says the LORD of hosts, the God of Israel: Houses and fields and vineyards shall again be bought in this land. (32:15)

See, I am going to gather them from all the lands to which I drove them in my anger and my wrath and in great indignation; I will bring them back to this place, and I will settle them in safety. They shall be my people, and I will be their God. I will give them one heart and one way, that they may fear me for all time, for their own good and the good of their children after them. I will make an everlasting covenant with them, never to draw back from doing good to them; and I will put the fear of me in their hearts, so that they may not turn from me. I will rejoice in doing good to them, and I will plant them in this land in faithfulness, with all my heart and all my soul. (32:37-41)

The poetry of welcome insists that the deep crisis of displacement is not the end of YHWH's dealings with Israel. The poetry shows us YHWH's resolve about the future, which in turn holds deep consequences for the present. As long as the displaced people are drugged by the ideological claims of Babylon, there will be no energy for departure and restoration. Thus this poetry of possibility serves to generate energy and courage to imagine and enact a future that the empire has sought to void. The poetry speaks in YHWH's voice in order to demonstrate that YHWH is the definitive player in Israel's future. Without the agency of YHWH (given in poetic imagination), there is no possibility of outflanking the ideological grip of the empire. The tradition of Jeremiah goes deepest into the heart of YHWH, there to disclose YHWH's resolve and anguish and wounded fidelity that become the ground for the future of Israel.

3. Isaiah

The poetry of welcome in Isaiah 40–55 comes later than that of Ezekiel and Jeremiah, and is better known among us because of

Handel's *Messiah*. In the final form of the text, this poetry obviously begins in chapter 40, just after the devastating prophetic oracle of judgment in 39:5-7. It is likely, however, that before we move from chapter 39 to chapter 40, we should first hear from the Book of Lamentations, for Isaiah 40–55 works best when understood as a divine response to the Book of Lamentations' deep grief over the destruction of Jerusalem and the deportation of folk from Jerusalem.[12]

The poetry of Isaiah 40–55 has the same intention as the poetry of welcome in Ezekiel and Jeremiah. It intends to evoke displaced Israel out of accommodation to Babylon, to move Israel back to its distinctive identity, and to authorize freedom and courage to return to Jewishness and to the land. It is like the traditions of Ezekiel and Jeremiah, except that it is more eloquent and more sustained, situated later in a somewhat different circumstance, and informed by a somewhat different memory.

This poetry plays against the hard unwelcome poetry of Isaiah 1–39, takes up many of the same themes, but now reverses course.[13] The initial word of "comfort" (Isaiah 40:1) is presented as gospel (40:9; 41:27; 52:7), as good news that is addressed to those settled in the bad news of the empire. The poet speaks an abrupt, reassuring, summoning word that opens the world to possibility for those who are able to trust in such words. Most spectacularly the poet says to the displaced:

> Do not fear, for I am with you,
>   do not be afraid, for I am your God;
> I will strengthen you, I will help you,
>   I will uphold you with my victorious right hand. (41:10)

> Do not fear, for I have redeemed you;
>   I have called you by name, you are mine. (43:1)

> Do not fear, or be afraid;
>   have I not told you from of old and declared it? (44:8)

There was plenty to fear in Babylon. There was taxation and exploitation, hostility toward local tradition, violence toward dissidents, and the requirement of conformity to imperial expectation. It was enough to cause the members of a local tradition to worry about opportunities for social advancement at the least, and perhaps even about their physical safety.

Knowing all of those fears, the poet speaks a word that voids them. The ground for fearlessness is the utterance, promise, presence, and resolve of YHWH. The "salvation oracle" is dominated by first person assertions by YHWH. YHWH enters the empire's affairs and overrides its threat of coercion, not unlike, of course, the way in which YHWH nullified the abusive authority of Pharaoh in ancient memory.[14]

The counterpoint to such spine-stiffening promises is the capacity to mock the empire in its empty pretension. Like every empire, Babylon was strong on posturing with its grandiose claims and projects. The poet, however, is unimpressed and dares to debunk the claims of Babylon. On the one hand, the mocking of empire directly concerns the arrogance of power in which Babylon imagined it was autonomous and could do whatever it wanted, with "no mercy." The claim of autonomy is everywhere evident in imperial conduct:

> You said, "I shall be mistress forever."
> . . . .
> [You] say in your heart,
>   "I am, and there is no one besides me;
> I shall not sit as a widow
>   or know the loss of children."
> . . . .
> You said, "No one sees me.
> . . . .
>   I am, and there is no one besides me." (47:7-8, 10)

But such claims cannot be sustained. And so the poetry moves on to YHWH's dismissive judgment on the empire:

Both these things shall come upon you
   in a moment, in one day:
the loss of children and widowhood
   shall come upon you in full measure. (47:9)

Evil shall come upon you,
   which you cannot charm away;
disaster shall fall upon you,
   which you will not be able to ward off;
and ruin shall come on you suddenly,
   of which you know nothing. (47:11).

See, they are like stubble,
   the fire consumes them;
they cannot deliver themselves
   from the power of the flame.
. . . .
Such to you are those with whom you have labored,
   who have trafficked with you from your youth;
they all wander about in their own paths;
   there is no one to save you. (47:14-15)

Autonomy is a lethal seduction for the empire because (so says the poet and so says the tradition) a holiness abides within human history that ultimately refuses such self-indulgence.

Beyond the dismissal of the human pretensions to power, the poet also directs sharp, biting words against the Babylonian gods who legitimate the economic-military enterprise of empire. These gods are impotent and have to be carried:

These things you carry are loaded
   as burdens on weary animals.
They stoop, they bow down together;
   they cannot save the burden,
   but themselves go into captivity. (46:1-2)

The contrast to YHWH is complete, for YHWH is a carrier who sustains on "eagles' wings" (46:4, see Exodus 19:4). In a mock

THE DIVINE AS THE POETIC

trial, moreover, the Babylonian gods are invited to give evidence of their effective goodness. But the invitation by the conjured judge is dismissive of the gods who can provide no such evidence:

> Let them bring them, and tell us what is to happen.
> Tell us the former things, what they are,
>   so that we may consider them,
> and that we may know their outcome;
>   or declare to us the things to come.
> Tell us what is to come hereafter,
>   that we may know that you are gods;
> do good, or do harm,
>   that we may be afraid and terrified. (41:22-23)

The verdict arising from the testimony (or lack of it) is inescapable. The gods—and their adherents—are nothing:

> You, indeed, are nothing
>   and your work is nothing at all;
>   whoever chooses you is an abomination. (41:24)

The poet delivers gifts to the listening, displaced Jews: assurance of YHWH's protection, and dismissal of the empire's phony claims to ultimacy. They are, rather, now freed and summoned out from the empire that is exposed as a fraud, a fake form kept alive and credible only by the management of imperial propaganda. The poetry tells us that the empire as ultimate authority is an illusion; only YHWH's reign is ultimately authoritative.

That new discernment summons the listening community to contrast dislocation in Babylon to the prospect of homecoming. The displacement features work that does not satisfy (55:2). The prospect of homecoming is anticipated in free wine and bread and water, given without cost (55:1). When the contrast is clear, Israel in exile is urged to convert (return) its sensibility. It is urged to recover its true identity as the people of YHWH, an identity that had been deeply compromised:

> Seek the LORD while he may be found,
>   call upon him while he is near;
> let the wicked forsake their way,
>   and the unrighteous their thoughts;
> let them return to the LORD, that he may have mercy on them,
>   and to our God, for he will abundantly pardon. (55:6-7)

YHWH offers mercy and pardon, gestures that never appeared in Babylon. The poetry presents the displaced community with a stark choice. For the poet, it is no contest at all; the alternative is obvious. The promise of YHWH is reliable (55:10-11). And so the displaced are imagined as departing the empire on the way home in joy and in peace:

> You shall go out in joy,
>   and be led back in peace;
> the mountains and the hills before you
>   shall burst into song,
>   and all the trees of the field shall clap their hands. (55:12)

All of creation will celebrate Israel's departure from the false promises of empire and back to the proper habitat of faithful covenant in Jerusalem, where dwells the God of fidelity.

In very different ways, these three voices of exilic possibility sound the theme of beginning again. Ezekiel in holy presence, Jeremiah in covenantal Torah obedience, and Isaiah with renovated Jerusalem all converge in the core claim. YHWH is back in play; and Israel can live again. YHWH is back in play, according to Ezekiel, because YHWH's recovery of reputation requires the rescue of Israel (Ezekiel 36:22, 32). YHWH is back in play, according to Jeremiah, because the father God anguished over suffering Israel (Jeremiah 30:20). YHWH is back in play, according to Isaiah, because YHWH could no longer be passive and silent (Isaiah 42:14). Holiness, fidelity, and eager resilience: with these accents the poets urged Israel to look beyond today's possibility toward what YHWH's resolve will accomplish tomorrow. Babylon is a pivotal place for such transformative, empowering poetry. It must be heard.

B. EMANCIPATORY IMAGINATION

This poetry to which the displaced listened raptly was a sustained act of emancipatory imagination. It empowered the Israelites to see YHWH as the one who would give them a new future out beyond the grip of Babylon. Such imagination debunked the theological claims of empire, and deflated the ideological hegemony of empire. Emancipatory imagination soars out beyond the facts on the ground.

It is not, however, to be taken as fanciful or unrelated to reality. Against the aphorism of Auden that poetry "does not do anything," this poetry of emancipation is deeply linked to political reality. On the one hand, such poetry arises from the beliefs of the community, and reflects ongoing political practice. On the other hand, such poetry generates, constructs, and authorizes such political practice. Thus the poetry, after being taken as imagination, must be seen in context as a sociological as well as an aesthetic act.

1. Ezekiel

Ezekiel, we know from the outset, was a priest (1:3). This fact led him to see the God-given future in a particular way. He is preoccupied with the issue of divine presence, and questions about how that presence can be properly hosted, and what circumstances and practices would evoke divine absence. Indeed, Ezekiel's famous initial vision of "the wheels" is a probe concerning divine presence in loci remote from Jerusalem, the proper place of presence.

Negatively, it is the practice of "abomination" that will offend YHWH and cause YHWH's withdrawal (8:6, 9, 13, 15, and 17).

The result of such an affront is that YHWH withdraws from the Jerusalem temple and, along with other displaced persons, comes to rest in Babylon (10:20-22). What interests us here, however, is the subsequent welcome poetry that imagines the return of divine presence to the temple and the reestablishment of the sacerdotal system that assures an abiding divine presence in the city. The sum of the imaginative literature of Ezekiel 40–48 concerns the return of YHWH to the Jerusalem temple, the reidentification of the temple as the source of life, and the reestablishment of the Zadokite priesthood as guarantor and administrator of the system:

> In Ezekiel 40-48 the post-exilic Zadokite leaders thus found a suitable blueprint for their restoration efforts. Moreover, the central theological theme running throughout Ezekiel's prophecies was embraced by the hierocratic leaders as most compatible with their own interests, that theme being the reestablishment within the nation Israel of a state of holiness conducive to the return of Yahweh to the midst of his people.[15]

Ezekiel 43:1-5 narrates the return of divine glory to the temple that had departed in chapters 8–10. The wonder of restored presence is that living water flowed out from beneath the altar to be life-giving and transformative for the entire ecosystem, not least the Dead Sea (47:7-8). In the end, the entire land is reckoned to be properly "holy," that is, suitable for divine habitation (47:13–48:35). The culminating affirmation of Ezekiel is that the new name of the holy city now restored is "The LORD is There" (48:35).

While this vision is wondrously vibrant in its imagery, we should not miss that the whole is properly ordered and guaranteed precisely by the priestly "descendants of Zadok" (44:15). The reference to the priests in chapters 45–46 leads to an inventory of holy regulations for the future. Thus the emancipatory literature has an eye on governance, power, and control, and envisions an authorized leadership with sufficient power to purpose and enforce nonnegotiable holiness in the community. The drift of the Ezekiel tradition is toward hierocracy, the rule of priests, anticipating and reflective of the role of priests in the postexilic community of restoration. The priests assured a holy people commensurate with a holy God.

2. Jeremiah

Jeremiah as well is identified at the outset as a priest, "of the priests who were in Anathoth" (1:1). While he shares with Ezekiel a generic identification as a priest, in fact his rootage is quite different from that of Ezekiel. While Ezekiel is of the Zadokites, the Jerusalem sacerdotal establishment with its accent on holiness, Jeremiah is from "Anathoth in the land of Benjamin," a rural priest of the northern covenantal tradition.[16]

It is evident that Jeremiah is rooted in and shaped by the covenantal tradition of Northern Israel that refers back to Moses and derives from Sinai. Thus the prose report of 11:1-17 portrays Jeremiah as an advocate of covenant; that covenant, moreover, places primary accent not on holiness but on neighborly fidelity that is concerned with the socioeconomic life of the community.

Two aspects of Jeremiah's social context are worth noting here. First, his associations with Baruch, son of Neriah (36:4), and with Seriah, son of Neriah (51:59), put him in touch with people tasked with making sure that the Torah scrolls were available, understood, and taken seriously. Second, he was connected to the family of Shaphan, who exercised considerable leverage in Jerusalem politics. Both groups stood opposed to royal policy in Jerusalem and viewed capitulation to and cooperation with Babylon as a wise political course that was, so they judged, the will of YHWH.

Jeremiah functioned, so it would seem, as the voice and point person for this counter opinion concerning policy in Jerusalem.[17] Note that this political realism about empire was also a powerful proposal for the future of Judaism. It saw restored Israel not as a major political force but rather as a community of intentional covenantal obedience that by its obedience received the protection and blessing of YHWH.

Such a view of historical reality could accommodate itself to imperial power, because the neighborly obedience of the covenantal tradition did not need to challenge in direct ways the claims and aims of empire. Thus in Jeremiah's vision of renewed covenant, the future is all about Torah obedience that is grounded in divine forgiveness (Jeremiah 31:31-34). It is likely the case that this tradition of restoration was carried by the "scroll people," the scribes, a movement that culminated in the leadership of Ezra the scribe (Nehemiah 8:1-8). It was this particular movement that helped to form Judaism as a "people of the book," as practitioners of the scroll. And the substance of the scroll is the narratives and commandments that attest to covenantal fidelity as the way to the future.

3. Isaiah

The tradition of Isaiah is not so easy to situate. But as Ezekiel features a *priestly holiness* and Jeremiah a *scribal covenant*, we may suggest that the poetic tradition of Isaiah is funded by a *vision of kingship* that moved easily between divine king and human king. In early Isaiah (First Isaiah), great attention is given to the Davidic kings in Jerusalem (Ahaz, Hezekiah), and the familiar poetry of 9:2-7 anticipates a future Davidic king. In 37:33-35, moreover, the city is saved, "for my own sake and for the sake of my servant David" (v. 35). But the Davidic claim is not overstated; for in 6:1-8, in his famous temple confrontation, it is at the death of the Davidic king that Isaiah has a vision of YHWH, the real king.

This double vision of divine king and human king is carried over into the Isaiah tradition of the poetry of restoration. Thus in 42:1-13, the poetry imitates the Psalms of Divine Enthronement as it celebrates the intrusion of the Divine Warrior into the life of the world. And in the breathless announcement of new rule in 52:7, the "good news" is the announcement that "your God reigns," or alternatively, "your God is King." The hope of the Isaiah tradition is the reentry of YHWH the King into international affairs in a robust and transformative way.

But the poetry is not finished with human kingship. For all its lyrical power, the welcome poetry of Isaiah 40–55 is realistic in its recognition that human history depends upon human agents. While there is allusion to YHWH's promise to David (55:3), in fact the poetry pushes in a new, quite surprising direction concerning human kingship. In 44:28 Cyrus the Persian king is reckoned as the agent of restoration in Jerusalem; and in 45:1, most remarkably, the same Cyrus is identified by YHWH as "his anointed," that is, "his messiah." Isaiah is able to transfer all of the authority of the Davidic tradition to this Gentile king, because he knows that human agency is the immediate source of historical transformation. The outcome of the Isaiah tradition is wondrously royal, a divine king dispatching a human king in the restoration of YHWH's kingdom of YHWH's people.

If we take these three great poetic traditions, we are able to see, in broad outline, that they variously advocate a future for YHWH's people that will be priestly, scribal, or royal. It strikes one that while these voices are agreed that it is the deep divine resolve that makes a future possible, that resolve is refracted through a variety of concrete images and metaphors that offer a variety of possible manifestations of Israelite restoration. It is not possible to "harmonize" these visions of the future because poets, in their concreteness, refuse homogenization. Rather, the tradition permits each such poetic voice to have its full, uncensored say. And we may imagine that various segments of the displaced community heard their favorite; the splendor of the tradition is that the listening community kept them all and permitted no single poetic vision to dominate its lore. While these visions—priestly, scribal, and royal—must have lived in some tension with one another, together they attest to the future that will be the inexplicable gift of divine transformation.

The realism of Jewish imagination recognized, in the end, that human agency is decisive. And that human agency, evoked by poetic emancipation, may take a variety of forms. But it must take a human form; it may be a temple (Ezekiel), a synagogue (Jeremiah), or a city-state (Isaiah). The merit of the poetry is to imagine well beyond imperial limitation. The displaced community is blessed (and no doubt vexed) by poets who refuse resignation and passive accommodation to the empire.

C. PROPHETIC VISION ROOTED IN NARRATIVE TRADITION

We may take one step further in appreciating the thickness of this welcome poetry for the community of the displaced. In addition to seeing the poetry linked to efforts at power concerning the control of the community (the point just above), we may notice as well that each of these poetic traditions of emancipatory imagination is rooted in and extends a narrative trajectory from pentateuchal tradition.[18] That is, the poetic voices under discussion are not ad hoc, but are rooted in, shaped by, and reflective of narrative trajectories in Israel that are regarded as deeply authoritative.

1. Ezekiel

The point is an obvious one with reference to Ezekiel. In imagining the new temple presence of YHWH in Ezekiel 40–48, the prophet repeatedly utilizes the term *holy*, that is, utterly devoted to YHWH. It is no accident that the other textual material that most prefers the term *holy* is the Priestly tradition of Leviticus.[19] At the center of that teaching is the command "You shall be holy, for I the LORD your God am holy" (Leviticus 19:2).

The cluster of commandments in Leviticus is designed to form and sustain a people suitable for YHWH.[20] Thus it is possible to see the emancipatory poetry of Ezekiel as an exposition of this deeply rooted passion for holiness.

2. Jeremiah

The case is similarly clear with Jeremiah and the covenantal traditions of Deuteronomy. Scholars have wondered for a very long time about the parallels and similarities between the two bodies of text. The older view was that Jeremiah was a "scissors and paste" editorial job to intrude Deuteronomy belatedly into Jeremiah. More recent work suggests that the relationship is an integral one, and Jeremiah is schooled in and reflective of the older covenantal tradition.[21] Thus Ezekiel and Jeremiah respectively reflect the twin traditions that dominate the Pentateuch.[22] They continue to extend those traditions to show how *holiness and/or covenantal fidelity* may be the characteristic marks of Israel in time to come.

3. Isaiah

The case with Isaiah is less clear. But given Isaiah's royal orientation with reference to David, and given the common assumption that the J (Yahwist) tradition of the Pentateuch connects the promise to Abraham to the fulfillment in David, it is not a great stretch to connect Isaiah to the J tradition. This linkage is further substantiated when it is recalled that it is the J tradition that most programmatically situates Israel among the nations, for it is Isaiah who has the international scene most clearly in purview.

Thus I suggest that these three great poetic voices of exile are correlated with the long scholarly identification of "pentateuchal sources," J, D, and P:

- Ezekiel and holy presence as in the Priestly tradition;
- Jeremiah and covenantal fidelity as in the tradition of Deuteronomy;
- Isaiah and a blessing to the nations as in the J tradition.

If this correlation of narrative sources and poetic voices is provisionally accepted, then it is clear that the Exile (or soon thereafter) became the matrix for the convergence of defining interpretive trajectories in Israel. The narrative claims of holiness, fidelity, and blessing issue, in poetic parlance, as presence, new covenant, and a light to the nations.

Two things become clear if we take these traditions all together. First, the tradition, all the way down, is pluralistic and allows for great freedom in the delineation of faith. The cluster of texts offers a wide range of legitimate ways in which to voice hope in YHWH. Second, in the framing of the tradition, no voice or narrative trajectory is permitted to defeat the others in the interest of a single, authoritative rendering. Perhaps that is what we might best expect in a community under pressure, a readiness to give room to others to voice the faith in a way that has compelling power for them.[23]

This latter point about pluralism all the way down and a refusal to allow a dominant voice a victory is an important one as we ponder the "local tradition" of the church in the U.S. empire. In recent religious discourse in the United States, the quarrelsome voice of sectarian exclusiveness has been sounded on all sides, left and right. But what could be more foolish (or unfaithful?) than to be busy excommunicating others in faith when the community is under deep imperial duress. The contemporary church amid empire may be instructed by the evidence of the Old Testament canon. It is apparent that Israel, in its displacement, did not push toward a monolith of faith or voice. Rather, it allowed immense diversity and freedom of articulation, surely recognizing a commonality of belonging, even with widely variant voices. It is in the nature of the poetic to permit other voices to stand alongside. But when poetry is misperceived as doctrine, the gracefulness of poetry is readily defeated by closure. A displaced community cannot easily embrace closure, for to do so is to replicate the lethal temptation of the empire in its anxiety. Empires seek closure, that is, a final interpretation. And final interpretations run toward final solutions. But the emancipatory texture of these displaced poets knows quite otherwise.

CHAPTER 5

CONTESTATION OVER EMPIRE

The LORD of hosts has sworn:
As I have designed,
   so shall it be;
and as I have planned,
   so shall it come to pass. . . .
For the LORD of hosts has planned,
   and who will annul it?
His hand is stretched out,
   and who will turn it back? (Isaiah 14:24, 27)

The discernment of the empire by adherents of the local tradition is characteristically tricky and ambiguous. In ancient Israel the reality of Babylon was overwhelming; it was not so easy or obvious to doubt or dismiss the Babylonian gods who appeared to be so powerful and effective. Thus even among the prophets we may observe an ambivalence that reflects political realism.

In the end, however, that courageous poetic tradition reached the conclusion that the empire was at best transitory and not to be trusted or feared. The theological grounding for this judgment is the undoubted sovereignty of YHWH over the nations; but that theological conviction was reinforced by the visible fading of the power of the empire. It is the assertion of YHWH's ultimate rule that clears the ground of fear, and opens the way for hope and new obedience. The capacity to offer a rhetorical assault against the empire and against the gods of the empire is crucial for the compelling force of the local tradition.

In parallel fashion, the local tradition of the church amid the United States empire is sure to share that same ambivalence about the empire, given tax exempt status and many other deferences. Theologically, however, the freedom and hope of the local tradition of the church depends upon trusting and saying aloud the conviction that the U.S. empire does not finally merit fear, trust, or eventually obedience. Such boldness is risky and not readily embraced by any of us. It is nonetheless crucial to see that the issue is elementally theological. The local tradition, when faithful, casts its lot with the one whose governance will not be "annulled."

In the preceding discussion, I have presented the Israel-Babylon relationship as definingly negative and adversarial. I have done so because that is the common and recurring view in Scripture. Israel's perception of Babylon begins in the experience of the empire as a *displacer*; all who belonged to Israel, those who were deported and those who were not, experienced displacement and readily identified Babylon as the agent of that displacement.[1] And from there the tradition used the term *Babylon* to refer to any antilife force that could be increasingly demonized in the imagination of the tradition.

Use the Israel-Babylon connection to understand the connection between the U.S. church and the U.S. empire, and that connection will once again be essentially negative and adversarial. When it is faithful to Jesus, the church will see the hegemonic economic-political-military-ideological force of the U.S. empire as destructive and eventually lethal. The first empire like this that the church encountered was Rome; small wonder that the book of Revelation employs the term *Babylon* to refer to Rome, or that the arrogance of Rome rivals that of ancient Babylon or the contemporary empire of the United States (Revelation 18:2, 21).[2]

The biblical literature characteristically employs an adversarial tone in referring to Babylon. But of course the facts on the ground are never as clear and simple as ideological passion may suggest. It was of course quite possible for some in the sixth century to find positive aspects of the power of Babylon, aspects such as its role as sponsor of international trade or as guarantor of an international order. Empires do have their use, and it is not surprising to find traces of affirmation about Babylon in the biblical tradition. Indeed, more than traces, for it could even be affirmed in ancient Israel that Babylon, in its imperial expansionism, was acting out YHWH's intention for the world and for Israel.

Thus we must allow for a sense of ambiguity and complexity about Babylon, because the empire may do good even as it is a devastator. Its reasons for doing good, of course, are never altruistic, but rather seek to further its interests and expand its power. Thus some in the ancient world saw that when Babylon imposed order on lesser states it also acted as their protector—albeit never a disinterested one. Indeed, some in Israel clearly perceived Persia, Babylon's successor on the world stage, as a benign or positive force. It is, moreover, well known that in the New Testament period one's status as a Roman citizen counted for a great deal (Acts 16:37-38; 22:25-29). And certainly in our own time, while we may discerningly critique U.S. imperial power, it is obvious that in many parts of the world—notably in Eastern Europe—the presence of U.S. assertive power is received affirmatively. Thus any critique of empire (Babylon, Rome, and the United States) must reckon with such affirmation.

It is not surprising, therefore, that the reality of Babylon, in its power and its assertiveness and its eventual demise, should be a focus of contested interpretive activity. That contestation concerned the reality of empire itself, the experience of Jews in their displacement at the hands of empire, and a wonderment about the rule of Babylon in a world known to be under the sovereign rule of YHWH. In order for the U.S. church to think well and faithfully

about the U.S. empire, we may consider this interpretive contestation in Israel's tradition, notably in the three poetic voices noted
above in chapter 4.

1 . EZEKIEL

Ezekiel of course lived and spoke during the time that Babylon
destroyed Jerusalem. He knew full well about the imperial devastation of Jerusalem. Indeed, he refers repeatedly to the coming of
Nebuchadnezzar against the city, and the consequent act of deporting the king from Jerusalem to Babylon (12:13; 17:12-20; 19:9;
21:19; 24:2). Babylon is the devastator! The only other usage by
the prophet concerns the coming capacity of Babylon to defeat and
destroy the kingdom of Tyre and the kingdom of Egypt (26:2;
29:18-19; 30:10, 24-25; 32:11). Thus Ezekiel fully acknowledges
Babylon's devastating capacity. But the language of Ezekiel is, for
the most part, descriptive without being interpretive. Ezekiel
knows that Babylon's role is decisive, but how he nuances that fact
is little explored in his utterances.

It is often noted that Ezekiel, in his Oracles Against the Nations,
has no critical word to speak again Babylon, nothing in protest of
the damage done to Jerusalem, nothing about brutality or arrogance or abusiveness (chaps. 25–32). While it is an argument from
silence, many often conclude that Ezekiel lives in and by the permit
of Babylon, and so has no critical word to speak against it. From
such a silence one might judge that Ezekiel had an essentially affir-
mative view of Babylon, concerning both the legitimate punishment of Jerusalem and the curbing of other threats to Judah. On
both counts, this silence may be reckoned as an affirmation of
Babylon, or at least a refusal to employ any adversarial rhetoric
against the empire. It may be that Ezekiel simply had a different
agenda. Or it may be that he gained from the beneficence of empire
and was not about to bite the hand that fed him. Or it may be that
mounting a critique of the empire was simply too dangerous. In

any case, Ezekiel makes clear that it is possible to be engaged with broad social issues without engaging in polemic against empire. That is an option most often not noticed in current critiques of empire, and an option that this writer is most inclined to disregard. But it is a genuine option, whether explained by appreciation or fear or focus elsewhere. The Ezekiel tradition does not treat Babylon as an adversary or as an inappropriate threat.

2. JEREMIAH

The matter is much more complex in Jeremiah. Jeremiah of course comments, as does Ezekiel, on the coming of Babylon (Nebuchadnezzar) against the city of Jerusalem.[3] He raises the ante, however, by identifying Nebuchadnezzar as a "servant of YHWH" who enacts the will of YHWH that Jerusalem should be destroyed (25:9; 27:6; 43:10). On this reading Babylonian expansion serves the purpose of YHWH. Thus far Jeremiah seems to agree with Ezekiel, and has intensified the rhetoric in a theological direction. As a consequence the Jeremiah tradition suggests that submission to Babylon is an act of faithful obedience, and resistance to Babylon is resistance to the will of YHWH:

> If you will only surrender to the officials of the king of Babylon, then your life shall be spared, and this city shall not be burned with fire, and you and your house shall live. But if you do not surrender to the officials of the king of Babylon, then this city shall be handed over to the Chaldeans, and they shall burn it with fire, and you yourself shall not escape from their hand. (38:17-18)

This verdict, in addition to prophetic passion, likely also reflects the pragmatism of Shaphan and his ilk who see that resistance to Babylon only brings destruction. The picture of submission and compliance is completed if we remember that Gedaliah, from the family of Shaphan, is the first Babylonian governor of Yehud.

Apparently these pragmatists anticipate that Babylonian policy would be friendly toward those who willingly surrendered:

> Do not be afraid of the king of Babylon, as you have been; do not be afraid of him, says the LORD, for I am with you, to save you and to rescue you from his hand. I will grant you mercy, and he will have mercy on you and restore you to your native soil. (42:11-12)

That is, YHWH's mercy toward surrendering Jews would be replicated by the mercy of the empire.[4] The prose tradition of Jeremiah can say this, even though the poetic tradition of Jeremiah has anticipated that the coming Babylonian army would show "no mercy" (6:23). And indeed, Jeremiah himself personally experienced such mercy from the empire (40:4-5). Perhaps the prophet extrapolates from his own experience of the empire, to expect a wider expression of the same generosity. Thus for a moment in the Jeremiah tradition the key players are all in sync: the sovereign will of YHWH, the anticipated policy of Babylon, and the confidence of the prophet. This convergence offers a positive regard for the empire. It is in this posture that Jeremiah wrote his famous letter to the first deportees in Babylon, urging them to settle there and to pray for the city of Babylon as the only route to well-being (29:4-7). Perhaps there is a good bit of realism in this counsel, for in fact the deportees had no other option. In any case, the prophet is able to entertain the prospect that Babylon might be a venue for the gift of shalom, even for the deportees.

But that moment of convergence cannot be sustained. YHWH's alliance with Babylon is a provisional one, dissolved by the recognition that the empire wills the local tradition of Judaism no good. The tradition of Jeremiah does an abrupt about-face. As it turns from judgment to hope, so it turns from affirmation of Babylon to an adversarial tone that grows stronger in the latter part of the book.

With that altered horizon, the Jeremiah tradition comes to

regard the Babylonian control of Judah's destiny as a deep misfortune, but happily a "short-term" misfortune. In the continuing tradition of Jeremiah, it is anticipated that Babylonian hegemony will be short-lived:

> This whole land shall become a ruin and a waste, and these nations shall serve the king of Babylon seventy years. Then after seventy years are completed, I will punish the king of Babylon and that nation, the land of the Chaldeans, for their iniquity, says the LORD, making the land an everlasting waste. I will bring upon that land all the words that I have uttered against it, everything written in this book, which Jeremiah prophesied against all the nations. (25:11-13)

> I have given all these lands into the hand of King Nebuchadnezzar of Babylon, my servant, and I have given him even the wild animals of the field to serve him. All the nations shall serve him and his son and his grandson, until the time of his own land comes; then many nations and great kings shall make him their slave. (27:6-7)

> They shall be carried to Babylon, and there they shall stay, until the day when I give attention to them, says the LORD. Then I will bring them up and restore them to this place. (27:22)

The double use of "until" in 27:7, 22 indicates that YHWH's alliance with Babylon cannot last. Very soon YHWH will turn against Babylon; the empire will be punished for "their iniquity" (25:12). The tradition of Jeremiah moves, as does the experience of the "local tradition" amid the empire. Pragmatism may have required provisional cooperation with empire. In the end, however, the local tradition of Israel cannot collude with empire precisely because YHWH, the God of the local tradition, is also the God of international politics who will not continue to collude with Babylon.

What is anticipated in the "until" assertions of the prose account is substantiated and filled out in the greet poem of chapters 50–51 to which allusion is made in 25:13.[5] As the culminating piece of Jeremiah's Oracles Against the Nations, the prophet celebrates the demise and destruction of Babylon. The breathless news for which the tradition has waited is that,

> Babylon is taken,
>> Bel is put to shame
>> Merodach is dismayed.
> Her images are put to shame,
>> her idols are dismayed. (50:2)

The city is conquered and the imperial gods are exposed as frauds. The agency of the defeat of the empire is Cyrus, a leader of "a company of great nations" stirred up by YHWH (50:9). Thus the tradition continues to assert that the great powers operate at the behest of YHWH, even if unwittingly. Indeed, the later tradition identified Cyrus as precisely the one anticipated and "stirred up" in 50:9:

In the first year of King Cyrus of Persia, in fulfillment of the word of the LORD spoken by Jeremiah, *the LORD stirred up the spirit of King Cyrus of Persia* so that he sent a herald throughout all his kingdom and also declared in a written edict: "Thus says King Cyrus of Persia: The LORD, the God of heaven, has given me all the kingdoms of the earth, and he has charged me to build him a house at Jerusalem, which is in Judah. Whoever is among you of all his people, may the LORD his God be with him! Let him go up." (2 Chronicles 36:22-23, emphasis added)[6]

The rise and fall of nations is at the behest of YHWH, and now it is time for Babylon to fall. The poetry spends little time cataloging Babylon's sins, although the arrogance of its assumed lack of accountability is an affront to YHWH (Jeremiah 50:32). This empire, like all empires, practiced autonomy and self-indulgence that eventually spent itself. The weeping of those in the local tradition (the Jews) evoked YHWH to act against the empire that in fact was not autonomous:

> "King Nebuchadrezzar of Babylon has devoured me,
>   he has crushed me;
> he has made me an empty vessel,
>   he has swallowed me like a monster;
> he has filled his belly with my delicacies,
>   he has spewed me out.
> May my torn flesh be avenged on Babylon,"
>   the inhabitants of Zion shall say.
> "May my blood be avenged on the inhabitants of Chaldea,"
>   Jerusalem shall say.
> Therefore thus says the LORD:
> I am going to defend your cause
>   and take vengeance for you.
> I will dry up her sea
>   and make her fountain dry;
> and Babylon shall become a heap of ruins,
>   a den of jackals,
> an object of horror and of hissing,
>   without inhabitant. (51:34-37)

This brief poetic oracle features the lament of Israel, an indictment of Babylon for self-indulgence ("filled his belly with my delicacies"), the petition of Israel for YHWH's vengeful action, and the resolve of YHWH to intervene decisively. The end comes quickly to the empire. And the empire, characteristically, is surprised at the ending because this empire, like every empire, has learned nothing in time. The prophetic tradition readily asserts that the empire is finally answerable to YHWH and never autonomous. And when it refuses such answering, dreadful demise happens. The tradition also knows to utilize the rhetoric of supernaturalism concerning *YHWH as the active agent* in the demise of empire. A closer reading of the poem, however, indicates that it is *human agency*, albeit at the behest of YHWH, that does the work of demise.[7]

Thus the Jeremiah tradition comes full circle from affirmation of empire (a view shared with Ezekiel) to judgment and rejection. Like every people oppressed too long, there is joy at the edge of gloating at the empire's rough demise.[8] As YHWH terminates the alliance with empire, so Jeremiah turns from talk of "mercy" and "shalom" for the empire to the reality of YHWH's dismissal of the empire: "When you finish reading this scroll, tie a stone to it, and throw it into the middle of the Euphrates, and say, 'Thus shall Babylon sink, to rise no more, because of the disasters that I am bringing on her'" (51:63-64).

Self-indulgent, arrogant autonomy cannot be sustained in a world answerable to uncompromising holiness.

3. ISAIAH

Ezekiel appears to be conventional in his assumption of empire; Jeremiah begins at the same place, but turns to negativity. When we arrive at the Isaiah tradition, we find nothing of affirmation. This tradition is consistent in its negative judgment concerning empire. It is possible to take the oracle of 39:5-7, at the close of First Isaiah, as a positive statement concerning Babylon, except that it is only descriptive and does not endorse the coming action of Babylon against Jerusalem. While negativity toward Babylon pervades the Isaiah tradition, we may focus on two extended texts that bespeak a critique of empire.

In Isaiah 13–14, chapters embedded in Isaiah's corpus of Oracles Against the Nations, the poetry anticipates the ferocious judgment of YHWH against Babylon that is to be enacted by the nations.[9] As is characteristic in such poetry, the accent is upon the punishment that is to come rather than upon any indictment that justifies the sure punishment. The indictment of Babylon, such as it is, concerns arrogance and the assumption of a godlike role in international affairs:

> You said in your heart,
>   "I will ascend to heaven;
> I will raise my throne

above the stars of God;
I will sit on the mount of assembly
  on the heights of Zaphon;
I will ascend to the tops of the clouds,
  I will make myself like the Most High." (14:13-14)

That arrogance, moreover, issues in policies of aggression and exploitation and brutality:

How the oppressor has ceased!
How his insolence has ceased!
The LORD has broken the staff of the wicked,
The scepter of rulers, that struck down the peoples in wrath
  with unceasing blows,
that ruled the nations in anger
  with unrelenting persecution. (14:4-6)

You will not be joined with them in burial,
  because you have destroyed your land,
  you have killed your people.
May the descendants of evildoers
  nevermore be named! (14:20)

The indictment is scarcely surprising. It consists in policies of violence that are essential to the establishment and maintenance of hegemony. But behind the policy is an ideology of autonomy that knows no curb on exploitation. In the prophetic calculus, the empire will be treated as it itself acted.[10] As the empire showed no mercy (Isaiah 47:6; Jeremiah 63), so the coming Persians will show no mercy (13:18; Jeremiah 50:42). The world of empire is void of mercy, because "mercy" arises from a sense of connectedness to the other. The empire, in its arrogance, acknowledges no such connectedness to anyone.

The second cluster of texts that may concern us is Isaiah 46–47. These chapters stand at the center of Second Isaiah, 40–55, a corpus that is preoccupied with Israel's emancipation from Babylonian imperialism. The demise of Babylon is anticipated quite explicitly in 43:14:

> Thus says the LORD,
>   your Redeemer, the Holy One of Israel:
> For your sake I will send to Babylon
>   and break down all the bars,
>   and the shouting of the Chaldeans will be turned
>   to lamentation. (43:14; see 48:14, 20)

The sum of the "gospel" in this poetry is that YHWH is effectively engaged in the overthrow of Babylon, so that the people of Judah can return home (40:9; 52:7). In chapters 46–47 in particular, the twin prophetic critiques concern *false theology* (46) and *exploitative policy* (47), which together provide the theological basis for the overthrow of empire.

Chapter 46 mocks and denounces the powerless and impotent imperial gods Bel and Nebo (46:1). Indeed, the gods of the empire are homemade commodities that have no power to save:

> Those who lavish gold from the purse,
>   and weigh out silver in the scales—
> they hire a goldsmith, who makes it into a god;
>   then they fall down and worship!
> They lift it to their shoulders, they carry it,
>   they set it in its place, and it stands there;
>   it cannot move from its place.
> If one cries out to it, it does not answer
>   or save anyone from trouble. (46:6-7; see 44:9-20)

By contrast, YHWH will do a new thing: dispatch Cyrus, "a bird of prey," to counter Babylon (46:11).

This polemic against Babylonian gods is matched in chapter 47 by a critique of the arrogance of Babylon as it claims autonomy:

> You said, "I shall be mistress forever."
> . . . .
> You . . . who say in your heart,
>   "I am, and there is no one besides me;
>   I shall not sit as a widow or know the loss of children."

. . . .
You said, "No one sees me."

. . . .
You said in your heart,
    "I am, and there is no one besides me." (47:7, 8, 10)

The upshot of such autonomy is an inability to show mercy, the very mercy that has been assumed in Jeremiah 42:12 (Isaiah 47:6). The outcome of such imperial arrogance is a sorry ending that is indeed willed by YHWH but enacted in the course of political history:

> See, they are like stubble,
>   the fire consumes them;
> they cannot deliver themselves
>   from the power of the flame.
> . . . .
> They all wander about in their own paths;
>   there is no one to save you. (47:14-15)

The empire is beyond saving, and the sovereign God is indifferent to its fate. The news from this poet is that the empire, which considered itself a permanent figure in the political landscape of realpolitik, is in fact a transient phenomenon, readily outlasted by the resolve of YHWH.

It is not possible to articulate a neat taxonomy of prophetic attitudes toward Babylon. But we can see a movement,

- from Ezekiel's *affirmation* of empire,
- to Jeremiah's *affirmation* that turns to devastating critique,
- and finally to *complete dismissal* by Isaiah.

This sequence suggests to me that the faith tradition of Israel has a strong propensity toward pragmatism. In some circumstances it is necessary to go along in order to get along.[11] Behind that pragmatism, however, is a durable theological conviction that regards the empire as secondary and therefore not to be excessively respected or embraced. Such a derivative status for empire depends upon the regular, recurring articulation of the ultimacy of YHWH. When Israel fails to remember, proclaim, and trust in YHWH's ultimacy, the empire occupies the vacuum and tries to claim that position for itself. The empire, moreover, wants to silence talk of YHWH and to occupy the space left by such silence. But the "local tradition," with its emancipatory imagination, regularly refuses such silence. Indeed, the local tradition can imagine YHWH refusing the silence urged by the empire in speech that causes transformation:

> For a long time I have held my peace,
>   I have kept still and restrained myself;
> now I will cry out like a woman in labor,
>   I will gasp and pant.
> I will lay waste mountains and hills,
>   and dry up all their herbage;
> I will turn the rivers into islands,
>   and dry up the pools.
> I will lead the blind
>   by a road they do not know,
> by paths they have not known
>   I will guide them.
> I will turn the darkness before them into light,
>   the rough places into level ground.
> These are the things I will do,
>   and I will not forsake them. (42:14-16; see 62:1)

CHAPTER 6

DEPARTURE FROM EMPIRE

A highway shall be there,
   and it shall be called the Holy Way;
the unclean shall not travel on it,
   but it shall be for God's people;
   no traveler, not even fools, shall go astray.
No lion shall be there,
   nor shall any ravenous beast come up on it;
they shall not be found there,
   but the redeemed shall walk there.
And the ransomed of the LORD shall return,
   and come to Zion with singing;
everlasting joy shall be upon their heads;
   they shall obtain joy and gladness,
   and sorrow and sighing shall flee away. (Isaiah 35:8-10)

The deepest theological conviction of Israel in exile is that YHWH continues to be faithful. The concrete consequence of that fidelity is that YHWH is resolved to bring Israel safely back to Jerusalem and to restore the shalom of covenant. This is a remarkable conviction, given the fact that imperial ideology always claims that there is not and cannot be life outside the empire.

It is precisely life beyond the reach of the empire, given in the resolve of YHWH, that is the core claim of Israel's hope. In order to give specificity to that claim, the poets of Israel offer imaginative scenarios of homecoming. In this instance, it is traveling on a safe "Holy Way," safe from the threat of ravenous beasts, all made in joy. The possibility of a new beginning of life in a safe place of promise, beyond imperial coercion, is the long-term hope of Israel.

In parallel fashion, the contemporary news of the gospel is that God invites and summons the faithful to a life beyond the demands and gifts of empire. In the New Testament, that offer is a call to discipleship. In contemporary practice, it is the joyous possibility of joyous existence beyond what I have elsewhere called the "therapeutic, technological, military consumerism" of our society. While the texts portray this homecoming as a joyous alternative, it is at the same time a costly alternative. Just as the erstwhile slaves in the book of Exodus yearned to return to Pharaoh's Egypt and just as many Jews preferred life in Babylon, so the imaginative possibility among us for an alternative life in the world is not cheap. But to "go out in shalom" is a mantra that continues to ring in the ears of those gathered in the "local tradition" of Yahwism.

The contestation between *empire* and *the local tradition of Israel* exhibits the complexity and ambiguity of faith in relation to hegemonic culture. Though the contest may have been vigorous and the rhetoric intense, the outcome was never in doubt. Exile is not home. Babylon is not and could never be the land of promise.[1] Thus the outcome of the contest—voiced in all three prophets we have mentioned—is that YHWH's chosen people in displacement must never sign on to the grip and ideology of the empire. As a consequence, this community with its peculiar vocation and identity always dissents from the empire's claims to ultimacy. Put more sharply, Jews must depart Babylon and return home.

There is no doubt that the master narrative of departure is the Exodus narrative (Exodus 1–15). The characters in that vivid encounter continue to reappear in the many replications of the narrative, always in new circumstances that juxtapose empire to local tradition. There is, of necessity, *always Moses*, a human agent who summons Israel to an alternative historical reality. There is *always Pharaoh*, who comes in many guises but who always seeks to reduce this peculiar people to a pawn in the large game of imperial production. And there is *always YHWH*, the God whose signature command to the empire is, "Let my people go" (Exodus 5:1). Most often the command is, "that they may serve me." Sometimes it is that "they may celebrate a festival to [worship] me" Either way, the summons subverts the empire's claim of ultimacy, reducing it instead to a recalcitrant vassal of YHWH. After the initial summons, the remainder of the Exodus narrative concerns a playful plot about the contest for power after the contest for authority has been resolved.[2] The outcome of the contest is that Israel sings and dances its emancipation en route to its proper, promised habitation (Exodus 15:1-18, 20-21). The culmination is a great doxology that asserts the abiding rule of YHWH, even over empire: "The LORD will reign forever and ever" (Exodus 15:18).

The penultimate verse in the celebrative doxology is an acknowledgment of homecoming, whether to the land or to the temple:

> You brought them in and planted them on the mountain of
>   your own possession,
>   the place, O LORD, that you made your abode,
>   the sanctuary, O LORD, that your hands have established.
>   (Exodus 15:17)

Israel continues to tell this story of departure and emancipation, to yearn for it in its present experience, and to replicate it in its liturgical performance (see Exodus 12:26-27; 13:3-10, 14-16).

The Exodus narrative of Exodus 1–15 no doubt continued to be edited and reshaped in the long traditioning process; and no doubt some of that continued editing occurred among the sixth-century deportees who are the subject of our study. But however the Exodus narrative reached its final form, clearly it gripped the imaginations of the sixth-century deportees. It became the master plot for those who viewed YHWH as the defining character in Israel's public history. All historical hope in ancient Israel was a retelling and a reperformance of that narrative. At the center of the narrative, moreover, is the bold, obedient act of departure, when the God who summoned to departure was embraced as stronger and more reliable than the gods (or the human agents) who sought to prevent departure.

1 . EZEKIEL

The corpus of Ezekiel is, in large scope, designed as judgment (chaps. 1–24) and restoration (chaps. 33–48). A close reading suggests, however, that the two themes of judgment and restoration—the dominant pattern of prophetic articulation in the sixth century—is pervasive in the literature and is not consigned only to those two large blocks of text.[3]

We may identify three patterned articulations of hope for the displaced in Ezekiel. First, there is a recurring assurance of "gathering the scattered" by YHWH. The God who dispersed in anger will restore in faithfulness:

> I will *gather* you from the peoples, and assemble you out of the countries where you have been *scattered*, and I will give you the land of Israel. When they come there, they will remove from it all its detestable things and all its abominations. I will give them one heart, and put a new spirit within them; I will remove the heart of stone from their flesh and give them a heart of flesh, so that they may follow my statutes and keep my ordinances and obey them. Then they shall be my people, and I will be their God. (11:17-20, emphasis added)

> They shall be secure on their soil; and they shall know that I am the LORD, when I break the bars of their yoke, and save them from the hands of those who enslaved them. They shall no more be plunder for the nations, nor shall the animals of

the land devour them; they shall live in safety, and no one shall make them afraid. I will provide for them a splendid vegetation so that they shall no more be consumed with hunger in the land, and no longer suffer the insults of the nations. They shall know that I, the Lord their God, am with them, and that they, the house of Israel, are my people, says the Lord God. You are my sheep, the sheep of my pasture and I am your God, says the Lord God. (34:27-31; see 37:12-14)

Two matters recur in these promissory passages. First, the act of restoration is unilateral. The oracles are declarations of YHWH's intent, almost completely without any imperative addressed to the displaced. It will be done *for them*. Second, the restoration is focused upon the reassertion of covenant and faithful reengagement with YHWH. The agenda of homecoming to the land is not absent, but it is subordinated to the renewal of the relationship.[4]

Second, in the three great historical recitals, the homecoming is the culminating event in the large narrative presentation in two cases. In Ezekiel chapter 16, the restoration concerns the covenant:

Yes, thus says the Lord God: I will deal with you as you have done, you who have despised the oath, breaking the covenant; yet I will remember my covenant with you in the days of your youth, and I will establish with you an everlasting covenant. Then you will remember your ways, and be ashamed when I take your sisters, both your elder and your younger, and give them to you as daughters, but not on account of my covenant with you. I will establish my covenant with you, and you shall know that I am the Lord, in order that you may remember and be confounded, and never open your mouth again because of your shame, when I forgive you all that you have done, says the Lord God. (vv. 59-63; see 20:34-35)

The purpose of the restoration is the resumption of worship and the exhibit of YHWH's holiness:

On my holy mountain, the mountain height of Israel, says the Lord GOD, there all the house of Israel, all of them, shall serve me in the land; there I will accept them, and there I will require your contributions and the choicest of your gifts, with all your sacred things. As a pleasing odor I will accept you, when I bring you out from the peoples, and gather you out of the countries where you have been scattered; and I will manifest my holiness among you in the sight of the nations. (20:40-41)

The outcome is restoration to land and to covenant:

You shall know that I am the LORD, when I bring you into the land of Israel, the country that I swore to give to your ancestors. . . . And you shall know that I am the LORD, when I deal with you for my name's sake, not according to your evil ways, or corrupt deeds, O house of Israel, says the Lord GOD. (20:42, 44)

In yet a third articulation, the departure from displacement features not the return of Israel but the return of YHWH to the temple in Jerusalem. This vision of return is a counterpoint to the departure of YHWH from Jerusalem in chapters 9–10. YHWH departs Jerusalem because the temple has become a profaned place where YHWH cannot dwell. Indeed, YHWH is forced out of Jerusalem because of the abomination of the place. When the holy place is purged, rebuilt, and restored according to the rigors of holiness, then it becomes again a fitting place as YHWH's habitat. In 43:1-5, the glory of YHWH returns to the temple, and in 44:1-3 the east gate of the temple is permanently shut; YHWH will not leave again. According to priestly imagination, the return of Holy God to the holy place permits the return of holy people to holy land. Having asserted YHWH's return to Jerusalem, the text can then go on to reiterate the borders and order of the holy land to which Israel will be restored (47:13–48:35). Thus the Ezekiel tradition envisions a departure from Babylon and a return home. But the entire matter will be a wondrous gift of YHWH. Note that

Ezekiel assigns no significant role to human agency here. Israel will simply find itself, by divine resolve, safely at home again.

2 . JEREMIAH

The tradition of Jeremiah continues Ezekiel's focus on the defining force of divine resolve. Again there is very little imperative addressed to Israel in its displacement. The rhetoric is much more an assertion of hope, inviting Israel to watch for and expect the emancipatory action of YHWH. Like Ezekiel, Jeremiah's purpose is to assure the displaced and to generate hope for a historical possibility that is grounded in divine resolve.

In the prose promise of Jeremiah 29:10-14, the accent is on YHWH's resolve, indicated by the series of first person pronouns. To be sure, Israel is expected to "pray and search," with the assurance that YHWH will be found. But the sentences anticipating Israel's action are completely embedded in YHWH's own action. Thus,

YHWH's action:	I will fulfill to you my promise and bring you back to this place. For surely I know the plans I have for you, says the LORD, plans for your welfare and not for harm, to give you a future with hope. (vv. 10-11)
Israel's action:	Then when you call upon me and come and pray to me, I will hear you. When you search for me, you will find me; if you seek me with all your heart. (vv. 12-13)
YHWH's action:	I will let you find me, says the LORD, and I will restore your fortunes and gather you from all the nations and all the places where I have driven you, says the LORD, and I will bring you back to the place from which I sent you into exile. (v. 14)

The decisiveness of YHWH's action is evident in the recurring phrase "I will restore your fortunes" (29:14; 30:3, 18; 32:44; 33:7, 11, 26). The action to come is genuinely transformative, and Israel is the blessed recipient of divine resolve (30:18-22; 31:3-5, 8-10).

There are, to be sure, expectations articulated for Israel. Thus in 31:4-5, "You shall take . . . you shall plant." And in 31:21:

> Set up road markers for yourself,
>   make yourself guideposts;
> consider well the highway,
>   the road by which you went.
> Return, O virgin Israel,
>   return to these your cities.

Israel is to take responsibility for the journey home. The double "return" in verse 21 leads to a reprimand in verse 22: "How long will you waver, / O faithless daughter?"

The verses suggest that there was reluctance and resistance on the part of the displaced, so that the unilateral resolve of YHWH cannot succeed without the positive response of Israel. And at least in this instance, the response of Israel was not glad and forthcoming. Thus we may see that Jeremiah edges away from the completely unilateral declaration of Ezekiel, but still regards the restoration and homecoming as a divine gift and accomplishment.

3. ISAIAH

When we come to the Isaiah tradition, the accent shifts noticeably. The difference may be a change from one tradition to another or, more likely in my judgment, the difference is because Isaiah 40–55 is later and is situated in a context of urgency wherein Israel surely must act. In the time of belated Ezekiel and Jeremiah, it was well to continue to generate hope so that the displaced did not regard empire as home. In that context, however, hope was remote from action, as there was no real viability for homecoming so long as Babylon maintained totalizing hegemony. But in the belated Isaiah poetry, geopolitics had exposed Babylon as weak, and it was for that reason that Jewish homecoming was a real historical possibility. As a consequence, the whole matter of homecoming shifts from the divine indicative to the human imperative. The divine resolve persists, but now it issues in urgent imperative.

We may detect in the belated Isaiah tradition a reluctance to depart empire. That reluctance is portrayed in the poetry as doubt about YHWH, but that doubt may reflect a coming to terms with Babylonian hegemony as normative and not to be questioned or resisted. Thus in 40:27,

> Why do you say, O Jacob,
>   and speak, O Israel,
> "My way is hidden from the LORD,
>   and my right is disregarded by my God"?

And again in 49:14: "Zion said, 'The LORD has forsaken me, / my Lord has forgotten me.' " (The same terms are reiterated from Lamentations 5:20.) The divine response in Isaiah 50:2, moreover, could suggest doubt about YHWH's capacity: "Is my hand shortened, that it cannot redeem?" (see 59:1).

These three texts suggest that when the time came to depart empire, when push came to shove, Israel's confidence in YHWH was not so strong as to overcome all fears of the empire. For this reason the poetry of Isaiah 40–55 (particularly the latter part) tries hard to motivate the displaced Jews with its sense of urgency and possibility.

While the poetry continues the declaration of powerful divine resolve, this poetry also teems with imperatives of summons. Notably Isaiah chapter 51 reads like a call to courage and resolve to act, in order to depart the empire. YHWH has taken all the prerequisite steps, but finally even the "unilateral" action of YHWH requires engagement and response. As though to overcome the paralysis of doubt and fear, the imperatives tumble out of the poetry:

> Listen. (51:1)
> Look. (v. 1)
> Look. (v. 2)
> Listen. (v. 4)
> Give heed. (v. 4)
> Lift up your eyes. (v. 6)
> Look. (v. 6)
> Listen. (v. 7)
> Do not fear. (v. 7)
> Do not be dismayed. (v. 7)
> Awake, awake, put on strength. (v. 9)
> Rouse yourself. (v. 17)
> Hear this. (v. 21)
> See. (v. 22)

The imperatives are, in almost every case, supported by motivational clauses that assure the displaced of YHWH's powerful fidelity.

The first verses of chapter 52 sound like a continuation of the imperatives of chapter 51:

> Awake, awake, put on. (v.1)
> Shake, rise up, loose. (v. 2)

These verses are followed by a prose passage that links the present departure to the ancient remembered Exodus (vv. 3-6). The double use of *hinnam* ("for nothing, without cause") suggests that the misfortune of Israel in displacement is without cause or merit, and will now be rectified.

The most explicit Exodus imperatives are in 52:11-12, where both the parallel and contrast to the initial exodus are evident:

> Depart, depart, go out from there!
> Touch no unclean thing;

> go out from the midst of it, purify yourselves,
>   you who carry the vessels of the LORD.
> For you shall not go out in haste,
>   and you shall not go in flight;
> for the LORD will go before you,
>   and the God of Israel will be your rear guard.

The departure from empire is as a holy people, uncontaminated by life in Babylon. This exodus departure, moreover, is contrasted with the original one "in haste," for now it is a safe passage completely protected by YHWH. Thus exodus from empire is like the Exodus from Egypt, except that this one is on all counts a better departure.[5]

The imperative "Do not fear the reproach of others" (51:7) calls to mind the several salvation oracles in 41:10, 13-14; and 43:1. The departing Israelites had much to fear in their refusal of empire. They had to fear the lethal force of empire just as had the ancient slaves. More than that, they had to fear that YHWH's resolve was not as good as YHWH's poetry, and that they would be abandoned "midstream," and left to the indignation of the empire. Thus the salvation oracles are not simply generic assurances; they are addressed precisely to the daring dissenters from empire. These assurances, moreover, echo and parallel the ancient "fear not" of Moses in the face of imperial force: "Do not be afraid, stand firm, and see the deliverance that the LORD will accomplish for you today; for the Egyptians whom you see today you shall never see again. The LORD will fight for you, and you have only to keep still" (Exodus 14:13-14).

Israel's act of departure, moreover, is taken by the poet Isaiah as a "witness" to the power of YHWH and as decisive testimony against the authority of empire. Thus in 43:10-13 Israel in exile is characterized as witness to YHWH, a testimony that may be offered in words but more likely is offered in bodily praxis. The designation as "witness" brings with it great risk, a risk countered by yet another assurance:

Do not fear, or be afraid;
　　have I not told you from of old and declared it?
　　You are my witnesses!
Is there any god besides me?
　　There is no other rock; I know not one. (Isaiah 44:8)

The juxtaposition of "do not fear" and "you are my witnesses" situates exactly the risk for the departees and the possibility of bold affirmation of YHWH in the face of the empire that has sought to eradicate the talk and force of YHWH.

Finally I read Isaiah 55 as a powerful and sustained invitation to depart. Verses 1-3 vigorously contrast life in the empire and life with YHWH. The latter is a life of free sustenance—no money, without price. The imperial alternative is labor that does not satisfy. The empire is always propelled by cheap labor. Because the empire provides neither material nor spiritual satisfaction to its laborers, the poet urges these workers to end their collusion with the empire.

The familiar summons of verses 6-9 to "seek YHWH" is not a generic summons to faith or to worship. It specifically summons the displaced who have lost their identity through accommodation to empire to reclaim that identity. The prophetic summons is to remember the peculiar identity that entails, perforce, repudiation of accommodation to empire. The "wicked" and the "unrighteous" are those who have forgotten their locus in faith, and have found easier, more accommodating ways to live. The news of the poetry is that those who have compromised will be received back into the merciful destiny of YHWH. YHWH has not rejected the compromisers, but they must return.

The ground for such a reengagement with the particular identity of Israel is that YHWH's word of promise is utterly reliable (55:11). The word that "will stand forever" (40:8) is the gospel word that YHWH is as powerful as a warrior (40:10) and as gentle as a shepherd (40:11) in bringing Israel home. In light of the summons (55:1-9) and the assurance (55:10-11), the poet concludes with a scenario of grand, majestic homecoming. The poet imagines a great procession—in joy and peace—that will be publicly observed and applauded, so that "all people shall see it together" (40:5). The intent of the poetry is to recruit listeners into the imaginative act of departure—from Babylon back to Jerusalem, from accommodation back to the specificity of Jewishness. For that imagery, the poet must inescapably utilize the metaphor of highway, a grand path leading home.[6] The highway back home is a safe path back to obedient existence and embrace of true identity. It is an image already offered in anticipation of Second Isaiah in 35:8-10:

> A highway shall be there,
>   and it shall be called *the Holy Way*;
> the unclean shall not travel on it,
>   but it shall be for God's people;
>   no traveler, not even fools, shall go astray.
> No lion shall be there,
>   nor shall any ravenous beast come up on it;
> they shall not be found there,
>   but the redeemed shall walk there.
> And the ransomed of the LORD shall return,
>   and come to Zion with singing;
> everlasting joy shall be upon their heads;
>   they shall obtain joy and gladness,
>   and sorrow and sighing shall flee away. (emphasis added)

The highway, moreover, is a metaphor reemployed in later Isaiah poetry:

> Go through, go through the gates,
>   prepare the way for the people;
> build up, build up *the highway*,
>   clear it of stones,
>   lift up an ensign over the peoples.
> The LORD has proclaimed
>   to the end of the earth:
> Say to daughter Zion,
>   "See, your salvation comes;

> his reward is with him,
>   and his recompense before him."
> They shall be called, "The Holy People,
>   The Redeemed of the LORD";
> and you shall be called, "Sought Out,
>   A City Not Forsaken."
>   (62:10-12, emphasis added; see Jeremiah 31:21)

Between the anticipation in 35:8-10 and the reuse of the image in 62:10-12, Isaiah 40–55 is bracketed by the highway in 40:3-4 and 55:12-13. It is all about joyous departure to true home.

When we come to think of faithful people in the U.S. empire, the transposition of the rhetoric of departure to this time and place is not an easy or obvious one; it requires some interpretive agility. It is beyond doubt that the imagery of these poets, and most particularly Isaiah, is geographical. The poetry imagines movement from one place to another. And if the poetry is kept with reference to geography, then it does not work in contemporary U.S. faith very well, for where would we go: New Zealand?

But it is surely credible to think that behind the geographical references there is a different kind of summons. The prior bid of the assurances of Ezekiel and Jeremiah and their summons to Israel is not primarily geographical. Rather, they remind their hearers that the YHWH story invites Jews to a special identity and a special role in human history. To be sure, geography is part of it, because the tradition cannot do without the notion of the land of promise. But to take the summons seriously does not require one to focus on its geographical dimension. And even if the geographical be taken as primary for Jews, it is clear that faithful Christians, as they seek to appropriate the text (and hopefully to do so without preempting it), read otherwise.

Thus this text summons Christians to depart the rapacious self-indulgence and exploitation of the U.S. empire, even as we continue to value and affirm this geographical space as our home. I suggest in such contemporary usage three dimensions of departure that belong to a faithful hearing of the text:

1. The departure from empire is *liturgical*, that is, it is a symbolic, bodily performance of what leaving is like. The accent on the liturgical is of course reinforced by Exodus 12–13 in which the Exodus memory is staged as a Passover liturgy designed for many replications in the service of sustaining distinct identity into the next generation. Christian liturgy, in U.S. empire, may be seen as a way of sustaining a peculiar (baptismal) identity that always seeks space for life outside the claims of empire.[7] The liturgy invites participants to recognize that we do not belong to empire and need not obey empire, just as African American liturgy demonstrates that the dominant culture does not "own" the black church and that African Americans do not "belong to Whitey." Such an awareness of the subversive edge of liturgy would require a deep rethinking of liturgical performance because much current liturgical performance assumes rather than subverts empire.

2. The reiterated practice of liturgical departure has as its intent a *psychological* transformation. The liturgy empowers participants to receive for themselves a different (baptismal) identity. Positively, this alternative self-recognition is to see one's self (and others in the community) as children of promise who live by the gift of God.[8] Negatively, such self-recognition may show us that we can live without the empire's gifts, that we can forgo the extravagances of consumerism, and that we need not aggrandize ourselves at the expense of the rest of the world. This new self-recognition may lead to what Augusta Neal has called a "socio-theology of letting go," a relinquishment of many of the gifts and enhancements that can only be guaranteed by empire.[9] The capacity for letting go is in the discovery that we need less, that everything we have is a gift that the empire cannot give, and that anxious self-advancement does not promote our well-being. The distinctive sign of that theology of "letting go" is no doubt the Sabbath that seeks to disengage, by bodily practice, the self from the imperial ideology of production and consumption.[10]

3. When the *liturgical* performance and *the practice of self-recognition* in the narrative of YHWH take hold, one can imagine that the departure from the empire is fundamentally an *economic* one, a refusal to participate in the aggressive economy of accumulation with all its practices of credit and debt. Clearly such an economic departure has profound implications; clearly as well, not many of us are prepared for those implications, just as not many in the ancient world of Israel were prepared to "renounce empire." But modest steps along the way to such radicality may open our eyes to further possibilities; and one never knows where the liberating presence of YHWH may lead. It is clear that a serious sabbath-practicing community would amount to a substantive defiance of empire.

I conclude this thought on departure from empire with three observations. First, the empire and its lethal commitments have a compelling capacity to draw us always again back into its grip. Thus Israel promptly and regularly wanted to return to Egypt, surrender themselves to Pharaoh's grip, and submit themselves again to his production quotas (Exodus 16:2-3; Numbers 11:4-5; 14:1-4). There is no doubt that "return to Egypt" is a recurring coercion for any who think to depart. Most tellingly, the concluding item in the long curse recital of Deuteronomy 28 is the ultimate threat of return to Egypt (v. 68). In the tradition of Jeremiah, when the fearful cannot think of anything else to do in their fear, they return to Egypt and take the reluctant prophet with them (Jeremiah 43). As with every addiction, we are endlessly drawn back into old habits of death that continue to exercise power. And of course the ideology of empire intends that any who dare to depart should sense themselves as deficient. That sense of deficiency is crucial in the compelling power of empire to draw us back to the additions of power and control.

Second, the compelling power of empire makes regular, reiterative narrative performance of emancipation in liturgy indispensable. Indeed, such liturgical performance is not unlike an AA meeting in which we meet together regularly to reiterate resolve to "stay on the wagon." Any perceptive departee knows, moreover, that failure to "make the meeting" will result in "falling off the wagon," back into the compulsions of empire. Thus liturgy may be seen, if faithfully construed, as an antidote to the assaults and seductions of empire.

Third, I find the summons and assurance of Isaiah 52:11-12 to be a most helpful focus point for the theme of departure:

- The initial double imperative is followed by ṣe'u, the most characteristic exodus term, meaning "go out." It is an imperative summoning to depart empire.

- The next line of the imperative asserts the holy vocation and holy identity of those who depart. While the mention of the "vessels of the LORD" suggests this was apparently addressed to priests who managed the liturgical hardware, it is important that the address is to a holy people, a people with an identity of singular loyalty and obedience to YHWH, without compromise. It is worth pondering the "unclean" things that would compromise such a holy identity. No doubt the term in context refers to the markings of empire that destroy holy identity.

- The third line of the poem reiterates the exodus imperative, "Go out."

- Verse 12 offers a divine assurance: The departure is not to be done "in haste" as with the original Exodus. Perhaps this is a pastoral recognition that it takes long, disciplined preparation to make a move of departure from empire.

- YHWH is the mighty protector who keeps safe from the threats and seductions of empire those who trust him. The poet imagines a joyous procession. This is not a mandate that coerces. The poet does not appeal to "the unwilling." The "relocation" is not understood to be a loss, for what is better than a journey to true identity, to come down "where we ought to be"!

CHAPTER 7

A Durable Metaphor . . .
Now Contemporary

Not with our ancestors did the LORD make this covenant, but with us, who are all of us here alive today.

(Deuteronomy 5:3)

The kingdom of the world has become the kingdom of our
    Lord
    and of his Messiah,
and he will reign forever and ever. (Revelation 11:15)

The Bible is no mere history lesson. Of course it reflects critically upon the past with a pedagogical intent. But if the Bible is the "Scripture of the church," then it is nonnegotiably contemporary in every time, place, and circumstance. It was the ancient practice of Israel to keep reusing and rereading and rehearing the old text in fresh and pertinent ways. The classic case of such reuse is the way in which the book of Deuteronomy represents the Sinai covenant to a new generation of the faithful. When we read the Bible as the Scripture of the church, we simply continue that ancient practice whereby we say, "The Word of the Lord . . . Thanks be to God." We purport to be listening for a contemporary word from God to us.

It is that contemporaneity that causes the metaphor to continue to be powerful in the life of faith. The generation of the faithful in Babylon reused old memories from Moses. The first generations of the church used the Babylonian memory of Israel in order to face up to the empire of Rome. And now, in our time and place and circumstance of empire, we may attend to the allusions to Babylon yet again, as pertinent to our faith and practice.

In ancient time and in contemporary time, it is the anticipation of the faithful that God's sovereign rule will become visible and effective in the world. We Christians end our most elemental prayer, echoing the doxology of Revelation, with the conviction "Thine is the kingdom and the power and the glory forever and ever. Amen."

In that familiar phrasing, we deny the claims of every empire, including the one in which we live. We "do time" there, but it is not our true habitat.

There is currently a great deal of ferment in study concerning the "Babylonian period" of Old Testament history and the circumstance of "exile."[1] This present study, however, did not arise directly from that current scholarly stirring. It was evoked, rather, by conversations with my Abingdon editor, Judith Pierson, concerning song lyrics by Emmylou Harris, Daryl Hall, and Jill Cunnliff titled "Time in Babylon."[2] Judith shared the song lyrics with me and we considered together the possibility of a study along those lines. While this study must, of necessity, take into account both historical data and the path of tradition, it has from the outset had an eye on contemporary life with a sense of urgency.

The song is organized in eight verses and three choruses. Each of the verses is in four lines; the choruses are in six. The reiterated refrain of each verse (except for verse 5) in the last line is "Doin' time in Babylon." The refrain in verse 5 is "Hard times in Babylon." Clearly each verse intends to place the listener in "Babylon." What strikes one about this reiterated placement in "Babylon" is that the intent and force of the song are quite

unmistakable, even though it offers no explanation for the reference and has no interest in historical questions about Babylon.

In this chapter I wish only to call attention to the metaphor of
"Babylon," both its constancy as a reference point for social criticism and its enormous flexible capacity to float with interpretive
power from one context to another. Clearly that constancy and
that flexibility are the work of the initial text-makers in the Old
Testament who, by the force of their imaginations, took what must
have been a routine and predictable imperial policy of deportation
and relocation and transformed it into a powerful and compelling
social commentary and summons. I have already cited the major
texts in the Old Testament portraying Babylon as a place of dislocation and as a place from which rescue will come. The name is
much used in historical texts as well as in the prophetic-poetic texts
I have cited. In addition I mention four other texts that show how
helpful a reference it can be:

- In Habukkuk 1:6 (here "Chaldea"), Babylon is raised by
  YHWH to assault Assyria. This is in line with Jeremiah's identification of Nebuchadnezzar as "servant of YHWH."
- In Micah 4:10, in a later elaboration in the poetry, Babylon is
  both the place to which "you shall go" and from there "you
  shall be rescued." The double usage is a summary of the "scatter-
  gather" pattern in Jeremiah 31:10, and summarizes the entire
  narrative of deportation and restoration.[3]
- In Zechariah the name occurs twice. In 2:7, there is yet again
  the declaration of rescue from Babylon; in 6:10 the oracle is
  addressed to those "who have arrived from Babylon." The
  two uses are consistent with the recurring pattern of deportation and restoration, though the accent is on the reconstruc-
  tion of the political economy of Jerusalem.
- In Psalm 87:4, we are offered a most remarkable use of the
  cipher. A safe, conventional reading is that Jews scattered in
  Babylon (and Rahab and Philistia and Tyre and Ethiopia)

should all look to Jerusalem as home. But Clint McCann offers a much more daring interpretation wherein the indigenous populations of those several states—including Babylon—themselves all look to Jerusalem as their home city . . . even though they are Babylonians!

The quotation in v. 4c is sometimes interpreted as something that individual Jews in the diaspora may have said as a matter of honor; however, it should not be taken so literally. Rather, v. 4 should be understood in the light of v. 6 . . . as the beginning of God's roll call of the peoples (on God's keeping records, see Exodus 32:32-33; Psalms 69:28; 139:16; Daniel 7:10; Revelation 20:12). In other words, the nations call Jerusalem their home (v. 4) because the God of Zion claims them as God's own people (v. 6; note that vv. 4c and 6b are identical). Actually, this perspective should not be as surprising as many commentators find it, for it is a recurrent claim that God's choice of Abraham and Israel meant that "in you all the families of the earth shall be blessed" (Genesis 12:3).[4]

On this reading the poetry goes well beyond a conventional focus on deportation of Jews and restoration of Jews, and imagines the ingathering of all nations . . . even including Babylon as a people of YHWH. McCann notes the parallel of Isaiah 19:24-25 where it is Egypt (Rahab) and Assyria who are named as God's people. Psalm 87 is an indication of the expansive potential of the metaphor of Babylon.

And of course at the historical end of the Old Testament is the Book of Daniel, which most scholars judge to be situated in the Maccabean crisis of 167–164 BCE. In the narratives of Daniel 2–4, Nebuchadnezzar is taken, on a critical reading, as a stand-in for the feared and despised Antiochus Epiphanus (see also Daniel 5:7; 7:1). In these narratives two matters recur. On the one hand, Nebuchadnezzar is ferocious, violent, and unrestrained. On the other hand, the wise Jew Daniel is capable of outflanking the Babylonian king and the entire Babylonian apparatus of intelligence. That is, the wisdom of the empire turns out to be inadequate if not foolish—and the faithful wisdom of this representative Jew prevails.

This variety of texts exhibits the ways in which the tremendous expansiveness of "Babylon" continues to feed and evoke the imagination of faithful Jews. They consistently recognized and affirmed both that the world of imperial power is a dangerous place and that the reality of the hidden rule of YHWH is more than competent to override the rapacious, exploitative claims of Babylon. The world in which both Babylonians and Jews must live is a dangerous world. It is, however, a dangerous world in which "help is on the way" that permits Jews to live a viable, safe, faithful life of mercy and righteousness. The imaginative capacity of these texts continues to insist that Babylon is at best penultimate in a world governed by YHWH. This is indeed "critical realism," realism about empire, but realism that does not give in.

The metaphor of Babylon is of course carried over into the New Testament where it serves as a surrogate for the empire of Rome that is viewed on occasion as the great enemy of God's rule, as "the great, mother of whores and of earth's abominations" (Revelation 17:5). The intense lyric of Revelation 18 celebrates the anticipated fall of Babylon:

> Fallen, fallen is Babylon the great! . . .
> Alas, alas, the great city,
>   Babylon, the mighty city!
> For in one hour your judgment has come.
>   (Revelation 18:2, 10; see 14:8)

The exposition of that fall is offered in two characteristic elements. First, there is *the indictment of empire*:

> As she glorified herself and lived luxuriously,
>   so give her a like measure of torment and grief.
> Since in her heart she says,
>   "I rule as a queen;

113

> I am no widow,
>> and I will never see grief." (18:7)

The core indictment concerns unrestrained, unlimited luxury that produced an arrogance that echoed the arrogance of Babylon in Isaiah 47:7-10. In its imagined autonomy Rome (Babylon) engaged in enormous self-indulgence:

> The merchants of the earth weep and mourn for her, since no one buys their cargo anymore, cargo of gold, silver, jewels and pearls, fine linen, purple, silk and scarlet, all kinds of scented wood, all articles of ivory, all articles of costly wood, bronze, iron, and marble, cinnamon, spice, incense, myrrh, frankincense, wine, olive oil, choice flour and wheat, cattle and sheep, horses and chariots, slaves—and human lives. (Revelation 18:11-13; see Isaiah 3)

> Alas, alas, the great city,
>> clothed in fine linen, in purple and scarlet,
> adorned with gold
>> with jewels, and with pearls! (18:16)

The commodity goods coveted by the empire are endless!

The second element, *the sentence of empire*, continues to reflect the luxury of Babylon (Rome) and the drastic end to that luxury:

> Her plagues will come in a single day—
>> pestilence and mourning and famine—
> and she will be burned with fire;
>> for mighty is the Lord God who judges her.
> . . . .
> With such violence Babylon the great city
>> will be thrown down,
>> and will be found *no more*;
> and the sound of harpists and minstrels and of flutists
>> and trumpeters
>> will be heard in you *no more*;

and an artisan of any trade
   will be found in you *no more*;
and the sound of the millstone
   will be heard in you *no more*;
and the light of a lamp
   will shine in you no more;
and the voice of bridegroom and bride
    will be heard in you *no more*;
for your merchants were the magnates of the earth,
   and all nations were deceived by your sorcery.
                (Revelation 18:8, 21-23, emphasis added)

The repeated "no more" of the end draws a line against Rome's (Babylon's) imagined autonomy. The indictment (couched as sentence) marks the vast commercial commitments of Rome that stood at the center of the world economy. Thus the empire stands under judgment by the familiar practice of autonomy, arrogance, self-indulgence, and greed. The poetry takes some delight in providing a complete inventory of consumer goods that reflect extreme consumer temptation, and then more delight in imagining the abrupt loss and the ready reduction of the empire to a "haunt" for every hateful beast.[5]

Note that Revelation's accent on commercial consumerism does not give much airtime to the drastic economic consequences of such luxury (the production of poor people) nor does it use much energy on the military spending and recruitment necessary to sustain such luxury, nor does it comment much on the theological dimensions of the extravagance. All of that, surely, is implied. But we should not miss the focus on the songs of lament and celebration. It is the characteristic self-indulgence of empire that brings an end.[6] Clearly for the Book of Revelation the community gathered around the Lamb in doxology is to keep itself remote from all such practices and seductions of empire.

Martin Luther famously took the metaphor of Babylon in a very different direction in his context, as an indictment of the hierarchy of the Roman Catholic Church of his time.[7] When I reread Luther's

"The Babylonian Captivity of the Church," I was surprised how little explicit use he made of the metaphor. Other than the title, he observes in his introduction, "I now know of a certainty that the papacy is the kingdom of Babylon and the power of Nimrod the mighty hunter."[8]

This opening verdict is a double hit. In addition to the figure of Babylon, the reference to "Nimrod the mighty hunter" leads to this proposition: The papacy is the mighty hunting of the Roman bishop.

By this Luther means that the papacy is an arena for plunder and confiscation and the seizure of prey. He does not say much more about his lead image of Babylon. But given Luther's critique of the opulence and self-indulgence of the papacy, he then proceeds in an extended and closely argued statement to consider the ways in which the sacraments of the church—the two principal ones and those he discounts as sacraments—have been distorted and abused by the papacy and robbed of their effectiveness as channels of free grace. The references to Babylon and its imperial practice pertain to the ways in which empires—in his read the Vatican as well—seize for their own use and purpose what is not rightfully theirs. It is of course to be remembered that Luther used his phrasing in the wake of the earlier crisis of the Vatican when, in the fourteenth century, the papacy was displaced to Avignon, reckoned to be captive to French politics. Of that moment in the papacy Kenneth Scott Latourette can write:

> In general, the Avignon years were marked by luxury in the Papal entourage and the enlargement of varied forms of Papal taxation and exaction. Palatial residences for Pope and cardinals were erected. These and the style of living maintained within them were costly. The Papal bureaucracy and the Papal ventures in politics also demanded large expenditures. Among the sources of funds were what were technically known as Papal reservation and provision. By reservation was meant the right of nomination to a vacant benefice. Provision was appointment to a benefice before it fell vacant. From each new appointee the Pope expected the annate,

approximately one year's revenue of the post. The income from vacant benefices the nomination to which was in Papal hands was also an increasing source of revenue, especially since the posts might be deliberately kept unfulfilled. In their effort to control the moral and religious life of Western Christendom the Popes, as we have seen, had encouraged or required appeal to their court. Under the Avignon Pontiffs the fees exacted for such appeals were another source of funds. These enlargements of Papal power and taxes aroused widespread resentment.[9]

Luther shared in being appalled at such self-indulgence. But his critique cut much deeper to the theological substance of the sacraments that had come to be used as source of power and control.

The most helpful comment on that "confiscation" that I know, lacking the theological density of Luther but alert to the primary issue, is that of Regina Schwartz, who observes that in earlier church usage the church was the *corpus Christi*, and the consecrated host of the Eucharist was termed the *corpus mysticum*. But by the twelfth century, she reports, "these meanings were reversed":

> The church, eager to assert the real presence of the human and the divine Christ against spiritualizing challenges, began to refer to the host as the *corpus Christi*, the body of Christ. That is, the term that originally signified the Christian Church then began to designate the consecrated host, and vice versa: the term used for the host, *corpus mysticum*, was gradually transferred to the Church. . . . To more fully grasp the course of sacrmentality, then, we must descend from the heights of mystical poetry to the depths of practical politics.[10]

The outcome of this reversal, Schwartz judges, is that:

> The Eucharist was given a strategic function: to consolidate the Church, by positing not just the equivalence but the identity between mystical reality and the visible and by making that depend upon hierarchical authority. Hence, the Eucharist

became a miracle made possible through the power of the Church—a power seemingly prior to the miracle. In this way, the Eucharist became a locus where the Church could exercise its control over the sacred. "This Eucharistic 'body' was the 'sacrament' of the *institution*, the visible instituting of what the institution was to become, its theoretical authorization and its pastoral tool." This co-optation of the Eucharist also vastly accentuated the institution's hierarchy, formalism, and legalism. The distinction between this later understanding of the sacrament and its origins is not trivial. It is the profound difference between a hierarchical institution appropriating the right to dispense the medicine of the Eucharist versus the belief that the Eucharist itself has the sacramental power to create a healthy social body. Mystery is the domain beyond human control, but here *sacramentality* (the Latin translation of the Greek *musterion*) is no longer contrasted to *instrumentality* for the mystery itself has been instrumentalized.[11]

This remarkable development transposed the Eucharist into a tool for political control, and of course the immense leverage— political and economic—that came with it. The capacity to utilize religious claims for the sake of political expansionism is a hallmark of empire. While Luther does not unpack the formula in that way, his use of the phrase "Babylonian captivity" rings true on that score. In empire—Babylon or any of its successors—everything is taken up in advancement for those who sit at the center of power. In his conclusion to his treatise, Luther comments upon the threats of the church against him and ends by quoting a hymn that refers to the "impious Herod."[12] Clearly Luther well understood the enormous power of the metaphor of empire, and makes use of it both for this theological argument about the sacraments and about his own vocation as a theological interpreter who stands against the awesome empire of his day. Finally, Luther stands before Emperor Charles, who stood with the church authorities who had sponsored his "captivity."

The metaphor of Babylon can shed much light on the lethal

underside of U.S. history and culture as well. Most recently Allen Callahan has gathered together remarkable resources concerning African Americans who have used the imagery to reflect on the racism and the institution of slavery that have shaped and distorted much of U.S. history.[13] Part of the power of the Babylon metaphor lies in its ability to empower resistance in new covenantal communities like the black church.

Now that we have arrived in our exposition at this contemporary usage of the biblical imagery of Babylon, we may return to the lyrics of Harris, Hall, and Cunnliff that evoked my study in the first place.

"Time in Babylon" invites and requires a careful reread of U.S. culture and history that refuses the common ideology and sloganeering of "democratic capitalism." This critique, since the collapse of the national economy, is made much easier and more obvious, because it is clear that the "democratic" qualifier to "capitalism" has completely disappeared. The widespread passion for "deregulation" has led to the unleashing of rapacious economic practices with a greedy appetite that has been eager to "devour the poor." What had passed for capitalist virtue is now readily exposed as a destructive selfishness that contradicts in wholesale ways any chance for the common good. So the lyrics:

Verse 1: Doin' time concerns an SUV, a speaker phone, and chrome. The passion is for big cars and a federal highway system and cheap gasoline, all markers of an insatiable power wrapped in speed and show, ever eager to get there first. Contrast Babylon's appetite for power and speed with the covenantal community that remains "in place" with neighbors, a practice embraced by the counterculture of monastic commitment to "place."[14]

Verse 2: The mansion is on a hill. The high ground bespeaks control and evokes the rhyming "pill." The capacity for technical medicine is available to serve every need, every ache, every deficiency, every risked pregnancy, so that we may be "ready when the time is right." Placed between "hill" and "pill" is an ironic use of

"Pleasantville"; the term not only rhymes, but evokes an *ersatz* Ozzie-and-Harriet telling of a simple time, a time marked by neither mansion nor pill. But now, on both sides of Pleasantville is the capacity to fend off the exigencies of reality, whether challenges from down below or risks from our own bodies, now either way completely safe.

Verse 3: A singe focus on the one-eye that shows all, television with its crass commercialism that robs soul and cheats dignity. The verse does not mention "survival shows," but that could be the next line, "survival" as an odd choice of words to exhibit raw competition that risks all against every neighbor.

Verse 4: The silicone reaffirms the imperial capacity for scientific renovation of the body, designed to resist mortality. But of course empire always acts to resist mortality. It seeks by its power, its buildings, its control, its learning to be immortal. Babylon could readily claim:

> I am, and there is no one besides me;
> I shall not sit as a widow
>   or know the loss of children. (Isaiah 47:8)[15]

And Rome could readily echo Babylon:

> I rule as a queen;
> I am no widow,
>   and I will never see grief. (Revelation 18:7)

Of course the U.S. drive of global militarism is to ensure uninterrupted life against every imaginable threat.

Chorus: The verse is irregular in its length of six lines and is thick with meaning that is not transparent. The opening "Little Boy Blue" I take to be a recruiter who is gathering and summoning and seducing "all our children." The pastoral quality of "crows are in the corn" might suggest a resistance to Babylon. But the next line turns on "kill" and so the recruiter surely looks for sons and daughters to be inducted into the killing fields. The crows are thereby transposed into vultures and buzzards waiting for carnage; and we are left with a residue of military devastation. The military is not like that on the surface. There it is all flag and bugle and parade and salute and bravery. But now we are underground: "underground in Babylon." We are underground when the PBS newspeople end each day in solemn silence to name the dead from the most recent harvest. We are underground when MSNBC can each night give the number of days (of killing and dying) since "Mission Accomplished." We are underground with amputees and mechanical body parts and homelessness and suicide and violence that must be financed for the next six decades. "Underground" is to take the steps from self-congratulation to the bodily reality that will not lie. It is no wonder that this verse is long and irregular, for military passion in empire is always long and not nearly as regular as we are wont to believe.

Verse 5: This verses returns to four-line regularity. We continue the theme of war with 'Nam. But in fact the verse exhibits all the wildness of the late 1960s–1970s: Watergate, the bomb, and civil rights. These images portray (depending on our point of view) either the social chaos exemplified by the 1968 Democratic Convention and the savage assassinations of that decade, or the prospect of a new society being born. Either way, the lines present a society that falls back on "apple pie and mom," but the fall-back options are remote from the crisis of the common good and from the facts on the ground. This inventory of upheaval would suggest that the empire cannot supply enough slices of apple pie to keep us from noticing the outcomes of the hurt. No wonder the last line, with a rhetorical departure, voices "hard times in Babylon"—hard times of uncertainty and violence and darkness, hard times caused by the reassuring refusal of Babylon to tell the truth or to face the failure.

Verse 6: The verse is a quick departure from the 1960s. There had been megaphone for crowd arousal and leadership. But now, concerning the megaphone, there is only, "Gave it up." Give up protest. Give up hope. Give up possibility. Settle for an easier agenda of shopping. Now the song moves toward expensive passions, an entry into a world of exotic pretend. Amid the most costly of Gucci creeds and their companionship with denial, there are no protests, no trials, no marches, no raw edges.[16] Now it is soft and private and expensive . . . not to worry!

Verse 7: These lines are quick. It's about money. Follow the money. It is indeed the economy . . . stupid! Empires are about money initially, amassing, leveraging. There is still a lot of it in some quarters, even after the collapse of much of it. The high end need not be restrained. Because the lines are still organized to deliver for the controllers who refuse socialism but in fact thrive on it . . . a free stadium, free use of taxpayer money for those who know how to access.

Verse 8: This final verse is couched as ironic cynicism, not really cynical. The lines invite to a surrender of soul. Surrender conscience! Pretend not to know. Eliminate the hard questions. Look out for number one. The body politic now is seen to be not more than an arena for private advantage. The poet is only catching up with the aggressive indifference of the action class.

The song is a wake-up call. The call is not that we should not go to Babylon; rather, it is to notice that Babylon is where we already are.[17] The claim, while familiar, is still alarming. We can scan the song for its accents: power, exhibit, entertainment, technological solutions, manipulation, recruitment, upheaval, fashion, selfishness. We can roll through the verses and through the themes. And then we notice. The cadences of Babylon do not necessarily add up to awareness. But they might. They might cause us to see—in sequence—*Babylon, Rome,* and *us,* and then notice that empires never learn. When we read from here to there, from the United States back to the Bible, we may discover that the durable urban cipher "city of Babylon" (see Jeremiah 29:7 on Babylon as city) comes with other urban figures. In the Bible Babylon comes with urban Jerusalem. Jerusalem is the city of the Great King, YHWH, who announces justice and who roars at injustice.[18] Jerusalem is the seat of God's deep promise of presence and well-being. Moreover, the unwelcome poetry of the prophets joins Jerusalem to Sodom:

> If the LORD of hosts
>   had not left us a few survivors,
> we would have been like *Sodom*,
>   and become like *Gomorrah*.
> Hear the word of the LORD,
>   you rulers of *Sodom*!
> Listen to the teaching of our God,
>   you people of *Gomorrah*!
>   (Isaiah 1:9-10, emphasis added)

> In the prophets of Jerusalem
>   I have seen a more shocking thing:
> they commit adultery and walk in lies;
>   they strengthen the hands of evildoers,
>   so that no one turns from wickedness;
> all of them have become like *Sodom* to me,
>   and its inhabitants like *Gomorrah*.
>   (Jeremiah 23:14, emphasis added)

And most poignantly:

> This was the guilt of your sister Sodom: she and her daughters had pride, excess of food, and prosperous ease, but did not aid the poor and needy. They were haughty, and did abominable things before me; therefore I removed them when I saw it. Samaria has not committed half your sins; you have committed more abominations than they, and have made your sisters appear righteous by all the abominations that you have committed. (Ezekiel 16:49-51, emphasis added; see Hosea 11:8-9)

The capacity of these poets creates lively possibilities:

- It seems a given to be "doin' time in Babylon";
- or perhaps more likely, we could be "doin' time" in Sodom;
- but by faith, we may be "doin' time" in Jerusalem.

In Jerusalem there is other work to do:

> For out of Zion shall go forth instruction,
>   and the word of the LORD from Jerusalem.
> He shall judge between many peoples,
>   and shall arbitrate between strong nations far away;
> they shall beat their swords into plowshares,
>   and their spears into pruning hooks;
> nation shall not lift up sword against nation,
>   neither shall they learn war any more;
> but they shall all sit under their own vines and under their
>   own fig trees,
>   and no one shall make them afraid,
>   for the mouth of the LORD of hosts has spoken.
>
> (Micah 4:2-4)

We will all undoubtedly be "doin' time." But the poets invite us to alternative times:

- The extravagances of Babylon;
- the predatory practices of Sodom;
- or the peacemaking of Jerusalem.

The fluidity of images suggests, given vigorous imagination, that the landscape can be read, described, and enacted alternatively.

But for now we are "doin' time in Babylon," recruited for the killing fields (chorus), narcoticized by apple pie (verse 5), with shelved consciences (verse 8). No wonder it is "hard times."

The durability of the image invites questions for those who stand in the local tradition of faith. What might we do while "doin' time"?

We might spend time in prayer for the city: "Seek the welfare of the city where I have sent you into exile, and pray to the LORD on its behalf, for in its welfare you will find your welfare" (Jeremiah 29:7).

We might confront and instruct the empire about the truth of governance: "May my counsel be acceptable to you: atone for your sins with righteousness, and your iniquities with mercy to the oppressed, so that your prosperity may be prolonged" (Daniel 4:27).

We might spend time remembering our true place:

> If I forget you, O Jerusalem,
>   let my right hand wither!
> Let my tongue cling to the roof of my mouth,
>   if I do not remember you,
> if I do not set Jerusalem
>   above my highest joy. (Psalm 137:5-6)

The reason for the urgency of remembering is because the empire specializes in forgetting. The empire intends to erase all local tradition and all local belonging and all local gospel. The most passionate of those doin' time in Babylon will refuse the amnesia that comes with wealth, power, and control.

But then . . . remembering also is not without its hazards. Indeed, the very psalm that exhibits the most resolved remembering is also the psalm that most craves vengeance:

> O daughter Babylon, you devastator!
>   Happy shall they be who pay you back
>   what you have done to us!
> Happy shall they be who take your little ones
>   and dash them against the rock! (Psalm 137:8-9)

These militant rememberers summon God also to remember, assuming that divine remembrance will lead to divine retaliation that takes the form of divine violence. Having done ample time in Babylon, Miroslav Volf ponders the cost and danger of remembering too much too long.[19] He offers a compelling riff on the fact that *forgiveness* is linked to *forgetting*, just as *vengeance* is linked to *remembering* too long. In the first instance, makers of empire forget and practitioners of local tradition remember, for how else to maintain local tradition?[20] In the elongated process, however, the matter is reversed. Empires remember everything; witness the oceans of records left by totalitarian regimes in which every affront and every enemy on the enemy's list is preserved to perpetuity.[21] Given such institutional, bureaucratic remembering, the local tradition of faith refuses the imperial practice: keep no police records in its heart. While Volf does not use our particular images, surely he would say that *forgetting* is the condition of *refusing empire*.

The matter is recognized in Isaiah to be dialectical. On the one hand, there is an urgency to remembering, to cherish the rootage that is deepest:

> Look to the rock from which you were hewn,
>   and to the quarry from which you were dug.
> Look to Abraham your father
>   and to Sarah who bore you;
> for he was but one when I called him,
>   but I blessed him and made him many. (Isaiah 51:1-2)

On the other hand, there is an urgency to forgetting in order to notice the newness:

> Do not remember the former things,
>   or consider the things of old.
> I am about to do a new thing;
>   now it springs forth, do you not perceive it?
>   (Isaiah 43:18-19)

126

Empires specialize in one-dimensional scripts. But the dissenting tradition is more supple than that. Such suppleness makes doin' time doable; empire becomes a context for generativity.

A final thought on this durable metaphor for our contemporary time. It may be that the United States as empire is a disputed point and not all will be persuaded. But here I suggest a test case: "You will know them by their fruits" (Matthew 7:20).[22] The proposition invites us to assess the fruits of U.S. empire, to see whether it is indeed an authentic empire. The fruits we might list that are positive include the maintenance of global stability and the investment of new wealth in developing cultures. These matters seem to depend directly upon the United States. But the ledger is not in balance if we consider the fruits of U.S. policy and conduct. The United States, in many important ways, is a predator economy that seizes resources, imposes a certain culture, does immense damage to the environment, and leaves many societies in poor shape by a pattern of intrusion and departure.

It is an enormous leap to the New Testament, but the Epistles' reconsideration of "fruits" falls within the midst of our topic. The Epistles delight to make contrasts between the old life and the new life in Christ:

> *The works of the flesh* are obvious: fornication, impurity, licentiousness, idolatry, sorcery, enmities, strife, jealousy, anger, quarrels, dissension, factions, envy, drunkenness, carousing, and things like these. . . . By contrast, *the fruit of the Spirit* is love, joy, peace, patience, kindness, generosity, faithfulness, gentleness, and self-control. (Galatians 5:19-23, emphasis added)

> They have lost all sensitivity and have abandoned themselves to licentiousness, greedy to practice every kind of impurity. . . . You were taught to put away your former way of life, your old self, corrupt and deluded by its lusts, and to be renewed in the spirit of your minds, and to clothe yourselves

with the new self, created according to the likeness of God in true righteousness and holiness. (Ephesians 4:19, 22-24)

Put away from you all bitterness and wrath and anger and wrangling and slander, together with all malice, and be kind to one another, tenderhearted, forgiving one another, as God in Christ has forgiven you. (Ephesians 4:31-32)

Put to death, therefore, whatever in you is earthly: fornication, impurity, passion, evil desire, and greed (which is idolatry). On account of these the wrath of God is coming on those who are disobedient. . . . But now you must get rid of all such things—anger, wrath, malice, slander, and abusive language from your mouth. Do not lie to one another, seeing that you have stripped off the old self with its practices and have clothed yourselves with the new self, which is being renewed in knowledge according to the image of its creator. . . . Bear with one another and, if anyone has a complaint against another, forgive each other; just as the Lord has forgiven you, so you also must forgive. Above all, clothe yourselves with love, which binds everything together in perfect harmony. (Colossians 3:5-6, 8-10, 13-14)

It is an enormous transposition to consider these inventories of the Epistles and to move them toward present-day questions of empire. Certainly an empire cannot be expected to replicate the marks of a faith community.[23] I believe, nonetheless, that the transposition is compellingly illuminating. There is no suggestion that the empire is satanic or demonic simply because it cannot make such a replication. But empires do thrive on practices that are inimical to covenantal righteousness. It is not difficult to see that the "fruits of empire" are indeed "greed (which is idolatry)."[24] The combination of military power, economic exploitation, indifference to environment, and a theology of entitlement generates antihuman values, policies, and practices. The community of faith, in the midst of empire, is called to a "more excellent way" (1 Corinthians 12:31), a way that consists in hospitality, generosity, and forgiveness.

The empire is an odd and hostile environment for such practice. But then, these fruits of faith are designed and summoned for precisely such a time and place and circumstance. The totalizing pageantry of empire always wants to think there are no alternatives to predatory power. But the community of faith always entertains an either/or that in time brings the community to the "cost and joy of discipleship." There is more than one way to "do time"!

CHAPTER 8

DOIN' TIME IN PERSIA

Thus says King Cyrus of Persia: The LORD, the God of heaven, has given me all the kingdoms of the earth, and he has charged me to build him a house at Jerusalem, which is in Judah. Whoever is among you of all his people, may the LORD his God be with him! Let him go up. (2 Chronicles 36:23)

Here we are, slaves to this day—slaves in the land that you gave to our ancestors to enjoy its fruit and its good gifts. (Nehemiah 9:36)

The promises of the great prophets came true! Babylon did disappear as a world power. Some of the Babylonian Jews did return to Jerusalem—enough to confirm the promises. The Babylonian environment that permitted Jews to contemplate homecoming was soon replaced by the long-lasting Persian Empire. The Persians did offer a more benign policy of permitting a Jewish homecoming. But in fact the reach of Persia was farther and longer-lasting than was that of Babylon. There would be no "going home" from Persia, for everywhere Jews went, including back to Jerusalem, it was still Persia!

As a consequence of this shift from Babylon to Persia, faith had to find other ways of being Jewish. In the Persian Empire, the exile-homecoming paradigm did not work well. In its place, the local tradition vis-à-vis the empire had to be one of accommodation and resistance; accommodation enough to survive and prosper, resistance enough to maintain a distinctive identity and ethic. This latter model required a kind of ability for the practice of the "Weapons of the Weak."

It is my thought, in this final discussion, that the faithful church amid the U.S. empire now needs not a model of "exile and homecoming" because the U.S. empire is everywhere. Rather, it requires the agility of "accommodation and resistance" that places a premium on shrewd intentionality. After the Persians issued the decree of homecoming, there was still oppressive, enslaving imperial service that required an alternative strategy. Current accent in Old Testament studies, I suggest, points to resources that only now have come into our purview. These texts offer a model of faithful agility, a model that may enliven and empower our own faithful intentionality.

Babylon stands at the center of the Old Testament imagination. Babylon is the goal of *deportation*, for the deportees arrived at the "rivers of Babylon" (Psalm 137:1). Babylon is, moreover, the place of strangeness from which the Jews *departed to go home*. Babylon as a metaphor gave shape to the dominant Old Testament interpretive pattern: much of the Old Testament is to be read in that light. It is evident, in retrospect, that this model for historical experience and interpretive practice is only one model alongside many others that were available. It is further evident that this model was imposed on the longer life of Israel, that this imposition was the work of a small group of deported Jews, and that the imposition of this model was a deliberate—and successful—effort to put forward this experience as normative for the larger community. Thus the model served to legitimate and enhance a group of returned exiles who came to exercise inordinate influence in the subsequent work of defining and sustaining Judaism.

That mode of *Israel amid empire* proposed a quite self-conscious community of faith that stood over against any imperial force. The sustained practice of "over-againstness" is what I have been expositing in the foregoing chapters. Israel in exile practiced resistance and defiance of empire, without which there would have been no subsequent homecoming. Indeed, we may imagine that this model was sponsored by and benefited an intentional group of fanatics who were able to maintain clear ideological distinctions without compromise or accommodation. The counterpoint to *imperial arrogance and self-indulgence* is *Israelite faithfulness and purity,* so that the relationship is a radical either/or of Babylon or Israel, with sharp, dismissive rhetoric.

This persistent characterization of Israel in empire is a spin-off of the core tradition of prophetic rhetoric. In the ninth through the seventh centuries BCE, the prophets directed their rhetoric against the Israelite dynasty and power elite. In the sixth century they used the same rhetoric, but this time turned it on the empire.[1] The prophets indicted the empire's arrogant autonomy that led inevitably to exploitation and brutality. The sentence the prophets pronounced on the empire was war and destruction, to be carried out by an unnamed historical agent. This prophetic rhetoric changes very little from the earlier cadences when it concerned only Judah and Israel. In the "classical Prophets" the indictment very often has to do with violations of neighborly Torah (or, alternatively, rules of purity); and the sentence recurrently was destruction, most often anticipated as enacted by a historical agent.[2] The experience of Israel in empire was a ready venue for the continuation of prophetic rhetoric that admitted no compromise with empire. The earlier prophetic word came to fruition in Israel's exile; the latter, in its restoration. Thus *prophetic judgment* and *prophetic hope* serve well the grid of "exile and restoration." The small community of exilic "hopers" made good use of radical rhetoric in a way that combined deeply rooted faith and powerful ideological self-promotion as the true carriers of faith and as the true agents of covenantal obedience.

The prophetic delineation of the historical crisis in the sixth century could not, on two counts, be sustained for very long. The first reason is historical: The Babylonian hegemonic power did not last very long. Nebuchadnezzar died in 562 BCE, and two decades of poor leadership, failed religious claims, and the rise of Persia to the east made the prophetic rhetoric against Babylon passé. The new circumstance of Israel under Persian hegemony evoked a very different rhetoric and a very different political practice.

The second reason this harsh either/or rhetoric could not be sustained for long, I suggest, is that the radical either/or of faith amid empire was not congenial to the facts on the ground even while the empire persisted. After the most aggressive prophetic rhetoric Babylon was, in fact, still there. The deportees still had to participate in the Babylonian economy. They still had to obey Babylonian laws, acknowledge Babylonian authority. After an orgy of radical rhetoric one must still "come to terms." And coming to terms required a different way in the world of empire.

The Persian Empire displaced the Babylonian Empire in short order and brought what may have been a new stance to imperial practice, even though the Persian Empire was still an empire and still acted like one. The different posture of Old Testament texts toward Babylon and toward Persia could hardly be more pronounced, even if the empires were in fact not that different. The dismissive polemics against Babylon have already been noted. Remarkably, there are no such explicit polemics against Persian rule in the Old Testament, not one. In part that may be due to the fact that Persian policy toward conquered peoples was very different, granting important dimensions of local rule. Thus Cyrus is reported to have permitted the deported Jews to return home (2 Chronicles 36:22-23). The Persians, moreover, were committed to funding the rebuilding of the Jerusalem temple. At the same time, these policies were especially favorable to an elite local leadership of Jews who knew how to curry the favor of the imperial government and how to take advantage of new policies for their own advancement. It is the case, moreover, that the formation of the textual tradition in the sixth century was likely the work of those who were most closely allied with imperial power and had the most to gain from it.

Thus the changed attitude toward empire arose partly from the empire's altered policy and partly from the Jewish leadership's calculated stance that sought to get what it could from the empire. For reasons that are quite complex, we can in any case note that the sharp metaphor "Babylon" is no longer directly in play. The long generative period of Persian hegemony produces no such compelling image, and so the rhetoric is not nearly as sharp as under the previous regime. For all of these reasons it seems right to judge that the militant model of *exile-restoration* is displaced by the more cagey, fluid model of *accommodation and resistance*, a model that required a great deal more agility.[3]

I have suggested that the prophetic rhetoric of the sixth century against Babylon has important continuities with earlier prophetic utterance. At the same time it is easy to observe that the tradition offers very little prophetic utterance in the fifth century, and none of it is aimed directly at Persia in the way that it was previously addressed to Babylon. I do not suggest that the near cessation of the prophetic in the Persian period was a large, intentional decision within Judaism. Rather, confrontational rhetoric, perhaps, turned out to be incommensurate with an environment that was on the face of it regarded as more benign. Thus it does not surprise that the preferred rhetoric of the later period was more likely to be sapiental.[4] It was a time when the shrewd pragmatism of wisdom teachers and the text-propelled imagination of the scribes displaced the more confrontational strategy of the prophets. While it is impossible to date or place the terse utterance of Amos 5:13, one can think it may pertain to this moment in the life of Israel: "The prudent will keep silent in such a time; / for it is an evil time."

Given the changed circumstance or the changed attitude to the imperial circumstance, it is at least thinkable that "prudence" led the wise to curb confrontational rhetoric for a more subtle strategy. The "evil time" may be pointedly the time after exile; or it may more generally be any time in which Israel is under an overlord and without freedom for its own life.

I suggest then that the texts reflect the change from a self-understanding of *exile-restoration* to one of *accommodation-resistance*. The change is to be understood in terms of the change of imperial overlords and a changed choice of rhetoric from confrontation to engagement. Above all, the change reflects the good sense of those more concerned with sustaining the life of the community than with being heroes. I will comment on four pieces of literature from the Old Testament that attest to the model of accommodation and resistance of the faithful in a colonial context.

1. EZRA AND NEHEMIAH

The broad historical data concerning Ezra the scribe and Nehemiah the governor of Yehud in the fifth century are relatively clear and beyond dispute. Nehemiah, as a political operative, exhibits the wisdom and prudence of a shrewd player in imperial politics. Nehemiah 1 helps to situate Nehemiah in relation to the residue of failed Jerusalem:

> One of my brothers, Hanani, came with certain men from Judah; and I asked them about the Jews that survived, those who had escaped the captivity, and about Jerusalem. They replied, "The survivors there in the province who escaped captivity are in great trouble and shame; the wall of Jerusalem is broken down, and its gates have been destroyed by fire." When I heard these words I sat down and wept, and mourned for days, fasting and praying before the God of heaven. I said, "O LORD God of heaven, the great and awesome God who keeps covenant and steadfast love with those who love him and keep his commandments; let your ear be

attentive and your eyes open to hear the prayer of your servant that I now pray before you day and night for your servants, the people of Israel, confessing the sins of the people of Israel, which we have sinned against you. Both I and my family have sinned. . . . O Lord, let your ear be attentive to the prayer of your servant, and to the prayer of your servants who delight in revering your name. Give success to your servant today, and grant him mercy in the sight of this man!" (Nehemiah 1:2-6, 11)

Nehemiah was a "cupbearer," a high official in the Persian Empire who had access to the ruler Artaxerxes. He knew, moreover, that he would have to deal with "this man" (v. 11). The ensuing narrative presents an exchange between ruler and cupbearer, between master and servant, and exhibits the shrewdness of Nehemiah before imperial power. The exchange of 2:2-8 permits Nehemiah to report to the king the desperate status of Jerusalem: "May the king live forever! Why should my face not be sad, when the city, the place of my ancestors' graves, lies waste, and its gates have been destroyed by fire?" (2:3).

Beyond the report, Nehemiah has positioned himself to appeal to the Persian king for credentials and resources:

"If it pleases the king, and if your servant has found favor with you, I ask that you send me to Judah, to the city of my ancestors' graves, so that I may rebuild it." The king said to me (the queen also was sitting beside him), "How long will you be gone, and when will you return?" So it pleased the king to send me, and I set him a date. Then I said to the king, "If it pleases the king, let letters be given me to the governors of the province Beyond the River, that they may grant me passage until I arrive in Judah; and a letter to Asaph, the keeper of the king's forest, directing him to give me timber to make beams for the gates of the temple fortress, and for the wall of the city, and for the house that I shall occupy." And the king granted me what I asked, for the gracious hand of my God was upon me. (2:5-8)

The outcome of this remarkable exchange has permitted Nehemiah to present himself completely subservient to Persia, and yet to receive funding and authorization for an ambitious Jewish project of rebuilding the city heretofore razed by the previous imperial power. Nehemiah has accomplished this by accommodating Artaxerxes with due deference and by acknowledgment that everything depends upon the goodwill and generosity of the empire.

After this initial credentialing, Nehemiah addresses himself to internal Jewish affairs and does not disturb the empire. Nehemiah would seem to be completely compliant to the empire; but he has received all that he asked and all that he needed in order to advance the well-being of the local tradition and to reestablish Jerusalem as a viable center of power and authority. Of course he does not go so far as to offer Jerusalem as challenge to Persia, but it is from his work that Jerusalem emerges as an alternative center of political gravity. Nehemiah's work is completely dependent upon the empire, but it is propelled by passions that are quite distinct from the interests of empire. The mandate of Persia to Nehemiah for Jerusalem, moreover, is reasserted and reinforced by Darius in the wake of Cyrus (Ezra 5:6–6:12).

In the case of Ezra the scribe, his work concerns the theological recovery of Jerusalem identity and the rehabilitation of Jewish religious practice. It is particularly important that he is a scribe, concerned with old traditions and memories that are to be revitalized. However a normative canon of Scripture came together, the tradition assigned Ezra a central role in that process.[5] The articulation and acceptance of an authorized (and authorizing) literature gave returning Jews and restored Jerusalem a clear, focused, and reliable identity. The public reading of the authorized scroll in Nehemiah 8, moreover, contributed crucially to the recovery and embrace of a distinct identity amid the empire. It is to be noticed that Ezra's accomplishment as a scribe in reasserting a scroll identity was done without any overt challenge to Persian authority. To that extent we may reckon Ezra, alongside Nehemiah, as an accommodator of empire. These men wanted only room for the articulation and practice of Jewish identity that did not need to disturb or challenge imperial oversight.

We may, however, pause over the prayer that is placed in Ezra's mouth in Nehemiah 9. For the most part the prayer follows the contours of covenant fidelity in terms of reciting YHWH's past graciousness toward Israel, acknowledging Israel's sin, and petitioning YHWH for fresh acts of grace and forgiveness. The prayer depends upon the righteous disposition of YHWH (vv. 8, 31, 33). The petition is, "Do not treat lightly . . ." (v. 32). We are, however, scarcely prepared for the way in which the prayer culminates. In verse 32 it is "hardship" that is the focus of petition. The prayer is not for forgiveness of sins, much as we might have expected that from the earlier verses. It is, rather, a prayer for deliverance from hardship. And the "hardship" is exposited in verses 36-37:

> Here we are, slaves to this day—slaves in the land that you gave to our ancestors to enjoy its fruit and its good gifts. Its rich yield goes to the kings whom you have set over us because of our sins; they have power also over our bodies and over our livestock at their pleasure, and we are in great distress.

The prayer no doubt makes a play on the double use of "serve": "They did not *serve* you" (v. 35); "Here we are, [*servants*]" (v. 36). Not faithful *servants of YHWH*; therefore, *servants of the Persians*! The specifics of "hardship" here concern the economic exploitation of Jewish agriculture to pay the taxes and tribute assessed by the Persian government. The power of Persia over "our bodies and over our livestock" (v. 37) is closely paralleled to the ancient memory of Egypt and dependence upon Pharaoh:

> Buy us and our land in exchange for food. We with our land will become slaves to Pharaoh; just give us seed, so that we may live and not die, and that the land may not become desolate. . . . You have saved our lives; may it please my lord, we will be slaves to Pharaoh. (Genesis 47:19, 25)

Indeed, that Genesis narrative may well reflect the context of fifth-century Yehud. Only now, in the prayer of Ezra, such economic enslavement is not welcome, but is a source of "great distress."

It is clear that Persian hegemony was seen to be heavy-handed and exploitative in a way that denied the citizens of Yehud the satisfactions of their own productivity . . . exactly what we'd expect from empire. With good reason, Blenkinsopp concludes: "It is implied, though of course not stated explicitly, that there was not much to choose between the Assyrians and their imperial successors, the Babylonians and Persians."[6]

The final sentence of Blenkinsopp concerning the prayer suggests a posture well short of accommodation: "The prayer is therefore, by implication, an aspiration toward political emancipation as a necessary precondition for the fulfillment of the promises."[7]

Now it may be judged that such a sentiment, safely hidden away in prayer, does not amount to any serious defiance of empire. Yet such an act, covert in liturgy, is nonetheless a venue for agitation and assertion of independent identity. It amounts to a "hidden script" that holds ominous political potential, and may be all that was possible in the circumstance.[8] The prayer in any case makes clear that Ezra, and likely Nehemiah as well, were not toadies to the empire who had abdicated their Jewishness. Their energy and passion concerned Jewish identity and well-being. We may believe they pushed this agenda as far as they were able, given that Persia was not as benign as its press releases suggested.

2. DANIEL

Scholars believe that the Book of Daniel was written after the Persian period, as late as the second century, BCE. But because the narratives make Nebuchadnezzar the symbol of imperial power, they demonstrate a recurring way for Jews to relate to empire. Thus while the narratives themselves (on either a traditional or a critical reading) do not pertain to the Persian period, they do exhibit the pattern of *accommodation and resistance* that concerns us in the Persian period.

Daniel 2–4 offers three narratives that present Daniel, the model Jewish practitioner of wisdom, as an effective operative in the empire. Because of the failure of "imperial intelligence" in the court of Nebuchadnezzar in chapter 2, the king intends to execute all of his wise men (2:12).[9] But Daniel, with "prudence and discretion," intervenes to save the Babylonian wise men (2:14); perhaps he shared a vocation and a practice with them, and so acted on their behalf.

In the narrative that follows, Daniel does what the wise men of the court could not do, suggesting that the capacity to engage the divine mystery is not situated in imperial chambers but outside of them amid the Jews! Daniel offers dream interpretations, that is, access to divine revelation. The impact of the dream, so says the Jewish wise man to the empire, is that "the God of heaven" (2:17, 19-21) raises up and brings down power (see 1 Samuel 2:6-8). This divine governance assigns penultimate significance to human forms of power (Daniel's present company included!), revealing the inscrutable ultimacy of God's own purposes. The dream interpretation evokes a theological affirmation from the king and a moment of pious submission to Daniel's God: "Truly, your God is God of gods and Lord of kings and a revealer of mysteries, for you have been able to reveal this mystery!" (Daniel 2:47).

Note the second outcome of this episode: Daniel receives promotion in the empire and creates space for his Jewish friends in the imperial apparatus (2:48-49). Finally, the narrative reports laconically, "Daniel remained at the king's court" (2:49). But he did so as an uncompromised Jew! He exercised his God-given gift of wisdom and bore witness to the ultimacy of his God. He did so in a way that the empire found praiseworthy and awesome. Daniel's covert defiance, dressed in conciliation's clothing, denied the ultimacy of empire.

A second narrative in chapter 3 moves in a quite different direction. Here the defiance of the three friends is much more direct.

The Jewish players in the story refuse to bow down to an imperial symbol. So it was reported to the king:

> There are certain Jews whom you have appointed over the affairs of the province of Babylon: Shadrach, Meshach, and Abednego. These pay no heed to you, O King. They do not serve your gods and they do not worship the golden statue that you have set up. (Daniel 3:12)

The refusal, moreover, is given bold theological grounding:

> O Nebuchadnezzar, we have no need to present a defense to you in this matter. If our God whom we serve is able to deliver us from the furnace of blazing fire and out of your hand, O king, let him deliver us. But if not, be it known to you, O king, that we will not serve your gods and we will not worship the golden statue that you have set up. (Daniel 3:16-18)

The confrontation leads to the contest of wills in the furnace of the empire (Deuteronomy 4:20) and then to the safety of the Jews:

> Nebuchadnezzar then approached the door of the furnace of blazing fire and said, "Shadrach, Meshach, and Abednego, servants of the Most High God, come out! Come here!" So Shadrach, Meshach, and Abednego came out from the fire. And the satraps, the prefects, the governors, and the king's counselors gathered together and saw that the fire had not had any power over the bodies of those men; the hair of their heads was not singed, their tunics were not harmed, and not even the smell of fire came from them. (Daniel 3:26-27)

Thus far this is a characteristic deliverance story that is free without explanation. It is, however, the recognition of YHWH that surprises:

> Nebuchadnezzar said, "Blessed be the God of Shadrach, Meshach, and Abednego, who has sent his angel and delivered

his servants who trusted in him. They disobeyed the king's command and yielded up their bodies rather than serve and worship any god except their own God. Therefore I make a decree: Any people, nation, or language that utters blasphemy against the God of Shadrach, Meshach, and Abednego shall be torn limb from limb, and their houses laid in ruins; for there is no other god who is able to deliver in this way." (vv. 28-29)

Remarkably, the king acknowledges the civil disobedience of the Jews: "They disobeyed." He recognizes, moreover, that the civil disobedience was in the service of their God, the God who refused imperial supervision. The royal decree that follows is a full recognition of the God of the Jewish defiers. And finally, the ones who disobeyed are "promoted" (v. 30). There is in this narrative no accommodation to the empire. It is all defiance without any smoothness; it is, in the end, defiance to which the empire can respond positively.

In the third narrative, in chapter 4, Daniel is again the dream interpreter. Again the text asserts the empire's secondary status, even going so far as to insist that the empire serves at the behest of God and will suffer "until you have learned that the Most High has sovereignty over the kingdom of mortals, and gives it to whom he will" (v. 25).

Beyond that verdict, and much more startling, is Daniel's readiness to give counsel to the empire in quintessential Jewish terms: "Atone for your sins with righteousness, and your iniquities with mercy to the oppressed, so that your prosperity may be prolonged" (4:27).

Daniel makes no concession to royal preeminence, but subordinates that arrogant imperial rule to the most elemental claim of the God of Sinai. It turns out, in this quick testimony, that mercy and righteousness—to the oppressed, no less!—is the wave of the future. Such a heavenly mandate violates and contradicts the most important passions of empire, for empires prosper primarily by exploiting the oppressed, transferring the wealth and well-being of the many to the few. The narrative ends with a moment of imperial sanity when even the great brutal empire can sing in Jewish cadences, almost as if converted:

Now I, Nebuchadnezzar, praise and extol and honor the King of heaven,
    for all his works are truth, and his ways are justice;
    and he is able to bring low those who walk in pride. (4:37)

The focus on truth and justice is the root of the issue between empire and local tradition. And the acknowledgment of "bring low" tells against all the hubris of empire (Luke 1:51).

When one asks where such courage to defy and such wisdom to accommodate come from, we are pushed back in the Daniel narrative—to chapter 1. There we are introduced to an earlier Daniel who is a recruit for imperial service, having been admitted to the training program for such service. The narrative turns on Daniel's refusal to eat the rich food of the imperial training table. "Daniel resolved that he would not defile himself" (1:8).That is, he would not compromise his identity by accepting the practices of empire that enact great self-indulgence. Instead of such rich imperial food he accepts a healthy Jewish diet of vegetables and water (1:12). The outcome is that at the end of the training period Daniel and his Jewish cohorts are "ten times better" than all the best that the empire can produce (1:20).

The accent on "being defiled" exhibits Daniel's Jewish resolve not to compromise his identity or conform to empire. That same refusal and resistance are evident in the narrative reference to his three friends. They are presented in the narrative, first of all, with Jewish names: "Hananiah, Mishael, and Azariah, from the tribe of Judah" (1:6).[10] The "palace master" renamed them to identify them not as Jews but as part of the empire. The effort is to eradicate Jewishness and to erase the long tradition of the colony. Remarkably, the narrative makes no comment on the act of renaming, and treats it as direct reportage. Nor does it make comment at the end of the narrative except to observe: "No one was found to compare with Daniel, Hananiah, Mishael, and Azariah" (1:19).

They are still Jews! They have kept their Jewish names! They have not given in. They are, nevertheless, "stationed in the king's court" (v. 19), and Daniel continued in imperial service. The act of defiance does not preclude effective presence in the empire.

I suggest that it is this initial act of self-identification placed first in the narrative collection that becomes the ground for all that follows. The initial refusal provided the grounding for the freedom and authority to come. What accommodation Daniel subsequently makes to empire is in the context of a fundamental defiance.

In his superb treatment of Daniel amid the Persians, Jon Berquist proposes that this Jewish narrative settles for piety as the clue for the future of Jewish life:

> What makes life is not one's political orientation or whether one serves the oppressor of Israel, but simply one's personal piety. Daniel maintains his integrity within the religion by focusing on regular and private acts of piety toward Yahweh. He keeps a kosher diet, despite the temptations of foreign food. . . . Thus the strategy for salvation in the narrative of Daniel is piety. Through observation of food laws and through regular, visible prayer, Daniel receives God's favor. This piety becomes the necessary mark of a faithful Jew when away from Jerusalem.[11]

There is no doubt that Berquist is right in this.[12] I do not think, however, that piety alone is the truth of the matter, as though a Jew, staying pious, could be uninterested in or disengaged from the larger world of politics. Certainly Daniel, in this portrayal, is not uninterested or disengaged. And indeed, his uncommon, God-given gifts assure that he would be drawn into political action that went well beyond piety:

- In chapter 2, he effectively communicates to the king that his power is penultimate;

- in chapter 3 the three friends refuse obedience to the empire and are promoted;
- in chapter 4 Daniel utters essential Jewish clichés and counters imperial temptation.

In all three narratives, this Jew models an active life in the empire that impinges in daring ways upon the course of the empire. There is no doubt that Daniel's daring refusal in chapter 1 is at the root of such conduct. But Daniel, as a model, refuses any quietism. This is a quite public Jew who enacts public Judaism in the empire. The narrative declares that Jews, even in their marginality, can make a difference in the quality of empire. The range of responses from defiance to wise counsel suggests that Jews engage empire with a thick repertoire of modes, a repertoire that can keep the empire off balance and open to surprise.

3. JOSEPH

While it is not certain that the Joseph narrative should be placed in Persian context (Genesis 37–50), the scholarly momentum is now moving in that direction. We may, in any case, take it in a Persian context, for the Joseph narrative, like the Daniel narrative, is easily transferrable from one imperial context to another. It is clear that the Joseph narrative is an account of how the "chosen people" made their way in an imperial environment, and von Rad has called attention to the sapiential dimensions of the narrative.[13] On those grounds, we may consider the Joseph narrative alongside the others I have pursued, as a study of the model of accommodation and defiance amid the Persian Empire.

In important ways, the Joseph narrative parallels the Daniel narrative. Like Daniel, Joseph is situated in an imperial regime that relies upon its own intelligence community. Like Daniel, Joseph faces a situation in which imperial intelligence fails (Genesis 41:8). Like Daniel, Joseph is a dream interpreter, is "discerning and wise," and is capable of giving good guidance to the empire (Genesis 41:33, which contains terminology similar to that in Daniel 2:14). Like Daniel, Joseph is inducted into royal service; Daniel's service fails to receive the same focus as that of Joseph's (Daniel 1:19-21; 2:28).

Given such parallels, however, we are also able to see that the Joseph narrative develops in a very different direction. Joseph, unlike Daniel, becomes a power player in the empire, and becomes the primary political agent under Pharaoh. More than that, he develops a food stratagem to the great benefit of Pharaoh at the dire expense of the subjects of Pharaoh. Given a food monopoly, Joseph, on behalf of Pharaoh, confiscates the land and the means of production of the peasants and reduces them to slavery (Genesis 47:19-26). The trajectory of Joseph's rise to power in Egypt has rightly been termed by Leon Kass the "Egyptianization" of Joseph: "Joseph uses his administrative authority to advance the despotic power of his master. Joseph's rise to full Egyptian power is, to say the least, highly problematic, both in itself and in its implications for the future of the Israelite way."[14]

In his account of Genesis 45, Kass comments:

> Pharaoh has in mind their assimilation into the land of Egypt, not their living apart in the land of Goshen. Three times Pharaoh mentions the land of Egypt, twice to offer up its goods. Whereas Joseph had urged his father to come with his flocks and his herds and "*all that thou hast,*" Pharaoh commands that only the people come, leaving their stuff behind. He pointedly tells them not to regret the abandonment of their own household goods ("your stuff" would include your pots and utensils, your clothing, and your instruments of worship), because they will be replaced by the best that Egypt can provide. Leave your ways behind, says Pharaoh. Become Egyptians, like Joseph.[15]

Kass's verdict is that Joseph is thoroughly "Egyptianized," and then he presses his entire people to become Egyptianized.[16]

The outcome of the narrative is that Joseph represents a model of *accommodation and defiance* that for the most part is very thin on defiance. The central theme is accommodation that brings with it enormous rewards and benefits for him and for his people. Of course we may make the argument that such a stance was required in order to save the people. Gerhard von Rad certainly made this argument by focusing on Genesis 45 and 50, to the almost complete neglect of chapter 47.[17] One could imagine that there were those who refused and disapproved such an accommodation strategy; but such disapproval only attests to the pluralism of which Judaism was capable amid the empire. In any case in the narrative as we have it, accommodation is the order of the day.

4. ESTHER

The book of Esther is the only part of the Old Testament that focuses completely on the reality of Persian power and the place of Jews in that empire. The narrative reports a life-and-death struggle for Jews that features the lethal contest between Haman and Mordecai as esteemed advisers to the Persian king Ahasuerus. The story unfolds as Haman plots to have all Jews in the empire eliminated, while Mordecai takes initiative to save them. Pay special attention here to the role played by the Persian king, who is above such quarrels and is assumed by all parties to be the ultimate authority on social transactions. That is, in the horizon of the narrative the fate of the Jews is fully within the scope and purview of the empire. There is no challenge to or questioning of empire.

The contest, under the aegis of the Persian king, pivots on the distinctiveness of the Jews and the maintenance or elimination of Jews. The key character is Esther, a niece of Mordecai who, by her charm and beauty, had become the new queen in the empire. The issue in the narrative is whether Esther would risk the exposure of her Jewish identity in order to save Jews or whether she would forgo disclosure of that identity in order to succeed in the world of

Ahasuerus. The plot is introduced when Haman resolves to "destroy all the Jews" (3:6). Mordecai counters that resolve by urging Esther to run personal risks for the sake of their shared Jewish identity, but also appeals to her own self-interest:

> Do not think that in the king's palace you will escape any more than all the other Jews. For if you keep silence at such a time as this, relief and deliverance will rise for the Jews from another quarter, but you and your father's family will perish. Who knows? Perhaps you have come to royal dignity for just such a time as this. (4:13-14)

Esther's noble, daring response signals the decisive turn in the narrative, and "the rest is history." Haman is exposed and executed, and the emperor provides decrees that permit the violent assertion of Jews against all their enemies in the empire. The outcome is the display of royal power in vigorous solidarity with Jews in their distinctive identity.

The crucial issue in the narrative is whether the exposure of Jewish ethnic identity is a viable way to be in the empire. Berquist comments:

> Esther faced a choice. Since her ethnicity was not widely known, she could have escaped the destruction planned for her ethnic group. To reveal her opposition to this plan could reveal her Jewishness, thus placing her at risk of her life as well. Mordecai encouraged her to prioritize her ethnic loyalties higher than her personal safety. This forms an integral part of the salvation for the entirety of the Jews. The story depicts ethnic loyalty as an essential virtue, overarching other values. Loyalty saves lives and produced a saved community that continues throughout history. If even one fewer person had been loyal in the past, the ethnic group might not have survived. . . . Thus the book of Esther presents a strategy for salvation as clear as those of the other short stories. Through the appropriate application of sexuality and through the high prioritization of ethnic loyalty, Esther cooperates with Mordecai and works through Ahasuerus to save the Jews as

an ethnic group. There are no limits to the exploitation of ethnic loyalty.[18]

The urgent teaching of the book of Esther is the urgency that Jewish identity must not be hidden. The book assures its readers that courageous self-assertion in the councils of power, albeit with studied shrewdness, will help win support and well-being in the empire.

A consideration of these four narratives indicates that Jews experienced a complex relationship with the empire, one that admitted of no single or simple solution. It is in any case clear that the shared assumption of these narratives is that we are remote from a model of *exile and restoration*. These characters are not going anywhere; they are not departing the Persian Empire. Rather, they must use their agility, shrewdness, and patience to come to terms with Persian power and mobilize that power to work for their own well-being. These narratives suggest a variety of modes of accommodation and defiance of empire.

- Ezra and Nehemiah mange to harness the resources and authorizations of the empire for local initiative; their hidden script emboldens them to tell the truth about imperial exploitation.
- Daniel, in his wisdom, moves from an initial act of disciplined defiance and exhibits enormous authority in rescuing the empire, having found ways both to defy and to instruct the empire.
- Joseph, at the other extreme, embraces "Egyptianization" (or in context we may say "Persianization"), whereby his Jewish identity is radically submerged in the management of imperial power and resources.
- Esther dares to exhibit her Jewish identity and wins over the empire to care for and protect her people.

The common theme is boldness, daring, and imagination that are to be enacted in a variety of strategies. All of these narratives underscore the importance of intentionality in the local tradition, and refusal to forgo that identity, though the refusal is perforce sometimes understated and opaque.

My thesis in these chapters has concerned "Doin' Time in Babylon." When we think of that theme in the U.S. church, we may think that the U.S. production-consumption system is an arrogant exploitation that invites denial among those on top and reduces all others to despair about ever producing or consuming enough. The image invites the church to confront the system with a prophetic edge, and with hope of restoration after the displacement of the system. The burden of this present chapter, however, is that for all the intense rhetoric of "Israel in Babylon," the Old Testament community did not and could not stay always with the courage of confrontation against Babylon and the rhetoric of exile and restoration. Both historical reality and psychological requirement moved the community from *exile in Babylon and restoration* to *accommodation and resistance in Persia.*

So now I ask, what is it like to be "doin' time in Persia"? And derivatively, "What is it like in the U.S. church when the model shifts from exile and restoration with its prophetic edge to accommodation and resistance with its wise realism?" The significant difference, I suggest, is that the image of "Babylon" proposes that the empire is intractable and cannot be affected. Conversely the model of "Persia," whatever the historical reality, suggests that the empire is not completely intractable, but that it can be moved by shrewd engagement. Thus the characters in the four narrative traditions I have considered—Ezra-Nehemiah, Daniel, Joseph, Esther—vigorously engage the empire and bring significant change. Now all of this is simply narrative imagination and, except in the cases of Ezra and Nehemiah, has no claim to be historical reportage. But even imagining that one's actions could have an impact on the empire is freeing, because such an act of imagination produces courage and staying power for the real world.

Given this "Persian" model we are invited to think of the church in the United States as a practitioner of "accommodation and resistance." I do not need to write much about accommodation in the U.S. church because we already specialize in capitulating and selling out to the dominant culture. Much of the church understands itself as a "voluntary association," a notion that brings with it little spine for resistance. And as Levenson comments concerning Joseph, "As always in Jewish history, the accommodation is dangerous and fragile and requires that the Jews be alert to the resentment that their differentness and their dual loyalties provoke."[19]

The church in the United States has largely signed on for democratic capitalism, and has watched while capitalism has been transposed into corporate socialism, while the democratic processes have been subordinated to the force of big money. The church has mostly positioned itself so that the promises of the gospel are readily lined out as "the American dream," with endless choices and bottomless entitlements that in turn have required the muscle of the military to sustain. The church, moreover, readily joined the generic uncritical assault on "communism" with a kind of laziness that refused social analysis. It is easy enough to see that on many fronts the assimilation of the U.S. church to empire requires a wholesale repentance.

But of course, we can and should think about those points at which assimilation to the needs and hopes of empire require accommodation because resistance without nuance leads to irrelevance and marginalization. If, however, we were to start thinking about resistance, then there would be much to say. Then we could look to the texts under discussion in this chapter and learn much from the refusal of the three Jews to bow down to Nebuchadnezzar and his statue: "These pay no heed to you, O King. They do not serve your gods and they do not worship the golden statue that you have set up" (Daniel 3:12).

This encounter is much more tenacious and direct than most of the other texts; it is an extreme case. Standing at the center of our model of resistance, this narrative invites us to ask just which embraces of empire entangle us in the worship of the empire's gods. It reminds us that our engagement with the empire can quickly become a case of the frog in the pot of boiling water. A little support of war, a little indifference about the environment, a little disregard of poverty, a little failure to notice racism or sexism, a little collapse of indignation and hope, a little innocence about class privilege; a little of this and a little of that, and all too soon comes a lethal society.

But of course resistance to empire in the U.S. church is nearly unthinkable, except perhaps in the most sectarian practices of peace churches or among Pentecostals. I know enough about the politics and economics of the church, especially local congregations to understand that the subject of resistance is beyond consideration. So what are the bishops, priests, pastors, and teachers of the church to do? Well, surely the beginning point is more faithful interpretation of Scripture with an informed hermeneutic that can let people see what is given us in "the news." A responsible hermeneutic for the church amid empire would teach us that social analysis is always taking place in Scripture. The texts constantly engage in the contest between power and truth-telling, a contest we would do well to join ourselves.

Such a teaching-preaching-interpreting enterprise would not, by itself, lead to the practice of resistance. It would, however, invite people to a fresh intentionality so that a decision about accommodation or resistance need not go by ignorant default, but could be considered knowingly. Against the fringes on the right and on the left of the church, it is possible, I have no doubt, to engage the broad body of the church in a sustained act of intentionality. Such intentionality would witness against the one-dimensional accommodation that is the temptation of the extreme Right and against the one-dimensional resistance that is the temptation of the extreme

Left. The outcome may be to see that the "Persian" practice requires an agility and an openness that lives in some hope for new possibilities out beyond ourselves.

Thus we may consider the lyrics by Harris, Hall, and Cunnliff one more time, with a turn to "Persian" accommodation and resistance. Such a modification of the lyrics beyond "Babylon" might recognize that "Babylonian" closure is reopened, and new possibilities are available. Empires thrive on the immutable "laws of the Persians and the Medes" (Esther 1:19). In Daniel 6, the issue of the immutability of empire comes to sharp focus. According to imperial edict, Daniel is required to die. And Darius, the Persian king, has no alternative but to implement the edict against anyone who prays to any other God. The king knows he cannot change what is immutable: "The thing stands fast, according to the law of the Medes and Persians, which cannot be revoked" (Daniel 6:12).

His advisers, against Daniel, know the same: "Know, O king, that it is a law of the Medes and Persians that no interdict or ordinance that the king establishes can be changed" (6:15).

And yet . . . ! In the exchange Darius hopes, against the edict, that Daniel will be saved: "May your God, whom you faithfully serve, deliver you!" (6:16).

And he is!

> Daniel then said to the king, "O king, live forever! My God sent his angel and shut the lions' mouths so that they would not hurt me, because I was found blameless before him; and also before you, O king, I have done no wrong." Then the king was exceedingly glad and commanded that Daniel be taken up out of the den. So Daniel was taken up out of the den, and no kind of harm was found on him, because he had trusted in his God. (Daniel 6:21-23)

The Persian king was "exceedingly glad" that the Jew was saved! The empire celebrates the rescue that the empire, perforce, was determined to resist. There are openings, even in empire.

We may, perhaps, read the lyric "Time in Babylon" "Persianly":

- Verse 1: Beyond trivial technology, there could be a pause in the rat race to get there first.
- Verse 2: Between the mansion and the pill, there could be attentiveness to human transformation that is not propelled by "bigger barns" and technical manipulation.
- Verse 3: The TV and its advertising liturgies could be put on "pause," a pause that refreshes!
- Verse 4: Instead of silicone and clone, there could be an embrace of mortality and love of the bodily self, even as we may love our neighbors in all their bodily reality.
- Chorus: There could be an alternative to the killing fields, with our children recruited as blacksmiths, designers of plowshares and pruning hooks. Such children could be "underground," peacemaking in ways that empires fear the most.
- Verse 5: Not learning war anymore, no more killing villages in order to save them, hard times become easy, human times.
- Verse 6: The dawning that "style" is imperial, a valuing of neighbor that forgoes consuming that is endlessly "conspicuous."[20]
- Verse 7: The awareness that being on the way is more crucial to human life than getting there first; cash now deployed so that the "have-nots" may be included among the "haves" and we need no longer be on the run.
- Verse 8: With conscience and self-awareness taken off the shelf and activated again with a passion.

"Doin' time" bespeaks prison. Doin' time in Babylon bespeaks imprisonment in a system from which there is no escape. But doin' time in Persia is different. It is not different because Persia will go away. It is not different because we will leave Persia, as there is no place outside "Persia." Rather, the difference is that the God of emancipation is at work, even transforming Persia. The prayer of

Ezra in Nehemiah 9 is "an aspiration toward political emancipation." In Daniel 6, even the Persian king can speak of divine deliverance.

And in another "Persian text," the poet can put it this way:

> The spirit of the Lord GOD is upon me,
>   because the LORD has anointed me;
> he has sent me to bring good news to the oppressed,
>   to bind up the brokenhearted,
> to proclaim liberty to the captives,
>   and release to the prisoners;
> to proclaim the year of the LORD's favor,
>   and the day of vengeance of our God;
>   to comfort all who mourn. (Isaiah 61:1-2)

The poem is the declaration of Jubilee in the midst of empire, the breaking of patterns of bondage and the cry of gladness and righteousness and praise. That freedom, in the "Persian" context, is perhaps not about going home. For wherever God's people might go, it would still be Persia. Rather, the new freedom, given by the mystery of God, is freedom to engage in accommodation and resistance. I have suggested a reorientation from the power of Babylon in its intractability to the power of Persia with its open possibility. It is a matter of editing the script of displacement; perhaps we may risk a slight revision of the famous "Serenity Prayer" commonly credited to Reinhold Niebuhr:

> Give me the dignity to accommodate,
> When accommodation is the only option;
> Give me the courage to resist,
> When identity depends upon it;
> Give me the wisdom to know when to resist and when to
>   accommodate.

I suggest a viable gospel posture amid empire. But as long as we are in an ideological posture to insist on a one-dimensional reaction to empire, there is no freedom. What happens with this freedom, embraced variously by the several textual witnesses, is that the law of the Medes and the Persians turns out to be supple and permeable. Even the king who champions the immutable law may be "exceedingly glad." The people of God in empire still are "doin' time." But all those times that we do in empire are in God's hand (Psalm 31:15). There is a freedom that the empire can neither give nor withhold (John 14:27).

NOTES

1. The Facts on the Ground . . . Twice!

1. See the stand summary of John Bright, *A History of Israel*, 4th ed. (Louisville: Westminster John Knox, 2000), 343–59. The "minimalists" views in current scholarship do not alter this picture much.

2. The tradition of Jeremiah reports a third incursion in 581, years after the monarchy had been terminated (Jeremiah 52:28-30).

3. See the classic statements on the matter by Peter R. Ackroyd, *Exile and Restoration*, OTL (Philadelphia: Westminster, 1968); and Ralph W. Klein, *Israel in Exile: A Theological Interpretation*, OBT (Philadelphia: Fortress, 1979); and more recently Daniel L. Smith, *The Religion of the Landless: The Social Context of the Babylonian Exile* (Bloomington, Ind.: Meyer-Stone Books, 1989).

4. Jacob Neusner, *Understanding Seeking Faith: Essays on the Case of Judaism*, vol. 1 of *Debates on Method, Reports of Results* (Atlanta: Scholars, 1986), 137.

5. Ibid., 138–39.

6. There can be no doubt that the "foe from the north" is Babylon. For other suggestions, see Henri Cazelles, "The Foe from the North," in *A Prophet to the Nations: Essays in Jeremiah Studies*, ed. Leo G. Perdue and Brian W. Kovacs, 129–49 (Winona Lake, Ind.: Eisenbrauns, 1984); and Brevard S. Childs, "The Enemy from the North and the Chaos Tradition," in ibid., 151–61.

7. This judgment is in the context of an awareness that there is more than one voice given airtime in the tradition of Jeremiah. See Carolyn J. Sharp, *Prophecy and Ideology in Jeremiah: Struggles for Authority in Deutero-Jeremianic Prose* (London: T. & T. Clark, 2003); and Christopher R. Seitz, *Theology in Conflict: Reactions to the Exile in the Book of Jeremiah* (Berlin: Walter de Gruyter, 1989).

8. See Robert R. Wilson, *Prophecy and Society in Ancient Israel* (Philadelphia: Fortress, 1980), 241–51.

9. On departure from Babylon as the new Exodus, see Bernhard W. Anderson, "Exodus and Covenant in Second Isaiah and Prophetic Tradition," in *Magnalia Dei, The Mighty Acts of God: Essays on the Bible and Archaeology in Memory of G. Ernest Wright*, ed. Frank Moore Cross et al. (Garden City, N.Y.: Doubleday, 1976), 339–59.

10. See James Boyd White, *Living Speech: Resisting the Empire of Force* (Princeton: Princeton University Press, 2006), on the force of language and the language of force in the empire.

11. On the lust for totality and alternatives to it, see Emmanuel Levinas, *Totality and Infinity: An Essay on Exteriority* (Pittsburgh: Duquesne University Press, 1969).

12. On that arrogance, see Donald E. Gowan, *When Man Becomes God: Humanism and Hybris in the Old Testament*, PTMS 6 (Pittsburgh: Pickwick Press, 1975); and most recently Neil Elliott, *The Arrogance of Nations: Reading Romans in the Shadow of Empire* (Minneapolis: Fortress, 2008).

13. See the summary survey of the great powers by Paul Kennedy, *The Rise and Fall of the Great Powers: Economic Change and Military Conflict from 1500 to 2000* (New York: Random House, 1987). For an amazing discussion of the great powers in the eighteenth and nineteenth centuries, see David Lawday, *Napoleon's Master: A Life of Prince Tallyrand* (New York: Harper, 2007).

14. I am using the phrase "local traditions" in a quite fluid way. I mean on the one hand to refer to the practice of the Christian Church as it lives in tension with the imperial ambitions of the United States. But I also refer, by the term, to local traditions of various kinds that do not readily assimilate to the dominant ideology of democratic capitalism. Such local traditions may be religious or ethnic and cultural or linguistic. The hegemony of the United States, like every such hegemony, is impatient with such dissenting expressions of identity and social practice.

15. On the reality of freedom for "local tradition," see John Witte Jr., *God's Joust, God's Justice: Law and Religion in Western Tradition* (Grand Rapids: Eerdmans, 2006). The most succinct statement on U.S. exceptionalism and its temptations known to me is by Gary Dorsey, "Consolidating the Empire: Neoconservatism and the Politics of American Dominion," *Political Theology* 6/4 (2005): 409–28.

16. The citation of Dorsey has behind it the work of Reinhold Niebuhr, on whom see Larry L. Rasmussen, "Reinhold Niebuhr," in *Empire and the Christian Tradition: New Readings of Classical Theologians*, ed. Kwok Pui-lan et al. (Minneapolis: Fortress, 2007), 371–87.

17. See James Bradley, *The Imperial Cruise: A Secret History of Empire and War* (New York: Little, Brown, 2009); and Walter Isaacson and Evan Thomas, *The Wise Men: Six Friends and the World They Made* (New York: Simon and Schuster, 1988).

18. It is commonly agreed that NSC-68, authored by Paul Nitze, provided the ground for the imperial policies of militarism and expansionism that unfolded in the next generations of American governance. See "Paul Nitze," *The Times* (October 22, 2004). One aspect of that was the containment theory of George Kennan, on which see *George F. Kennan and John Lukacs, George F. Kennan and the Origins of Containment, 1944–1946: The Kennan-Lukacs Correspondence* (Columbia: University of Missouri Press, 1997).

19. The celebration of that "victory" was given classic expression by Francis Fukuyama, *The End of History and the Last Man* (New York: Free Press, 1992). Happily, Fukuyama has since then repudiated the argument and the conclusion that he had drawn. Of course the facts on the ground in any case have contradicted his judgment.

20. See a defense of such policy by Josef Joffe, *Überpower: The Imperial Temptation of America* (New York: Norton, 2006). Even though his title alludes to the temptation, his discussion suggests the wisdom of yielding to the temptation.

21. On the one hand, Fareed Zakaria, *The Post-American World* (New York: Norton, 2008); and Martin Jacques, *When China Rules the World: The End of the Western World and the Birth of a New Global Order* (New York: Penguin, 2009), soberly look at the rise of challenges to U.S. hegemony. On the other hand, Thomas P. M. Barnett, *Great Powers: America and the World After Bush* (New York: Putnam, 2009), only wants to make adjustments in order to maintain that hegemony. We are only at the beginning of that conversation, one that will impinge mightily upon the governance of Barak Obama.

2. Awaiting Babylon

1. See Walter Brueggemann, "Always in the Shadow of the Empire," *The Church As Counterculture*, ed. Michael L. Budde and Robert W. Brimlow (Albany: SUNY Press, 2000), 39–58.

2. The Priestly tradition in particular is not much interested in the context of empire. Curiously in one place, Exodus 29:6, even the Priestly tradition makes the connection to the regime of Pharaoh.

3. See Walter Brueggemann, *Solomon: Israel's Ironic Icon of Human Achievement* (Columbia: University of South Carolina Press, 2005).

4. This is particularly the case with the holiness disciplines of the Priestly tradition; see John G. Gammie, *Holiness in Israel*, OBT

(Minneapolis: Fortress, 1989), 9–70. On the contemporaneity of these traditions, see the remarkable statement of Michael Fishbane, *Sacred Attunement: A Jewish Theology* (Chicago: University of Chicago Press, 2008).

5. Norman K. Gottwald, *All the Kingdoms of the Earth: Israelite Prophecy and International Relations in the Ancient Near East* (New York: Harper & Row, 1964), has provided a full review of the materials. Gottwald confines himself to historical questions but provides the basis for moving the topic in more metaphorical directions.

6. Klaus Koch, *The Prophets*, vol. 1, *The Assyrian Period* (Philadelphia: Fortress, 1983), 5, 73, 88, 156, and passim. It is YHWH who "arouses" and "stirs up" Cyrus (Isaiah 41:2, 25); the divine action is "meta" in that Cyrus is mobilized by YHWH, though "you do not know me" (Isaiah 45:5).

7. Here I take a conventional correction of the text.

8. The matter of divine agency and cause is a complex one, one on which I have learned a great deal from Terence Fretheim. See the discussion of the issue under the rubric of "instigator" by David Daube, *David Daube's Gifford Lectures*, vol. 1, *The Deed & the Doer in the Bible*, ed. and comp. Calum Carmichael (West Conshohocken, Pa.: Templeton Foundation Press), 131–49.

9. See John Hill, *Friend or Foe? The Figure of Babylon in the Book of Jeremiah MT*, BibInt (Leiden: Brill, 1999).

10. The parallel to Jeremiah in Isaiah 36–37 concerns the way in which Assyria claims to have been dispatched by YHWH; on the critical questions with this text, see Brevard S. Childs, *Isaiah and the Assyrian Crisis* (Naperville, Ill.: Allenson, 1967).

11. See Claus Westermann, *Basic Forms of Prophetic Speech* (Philadelphia: Westminster, 1967).

12. Gunnar Myrdal, *An American Dilemma: The Negro Problem and Modern Democracy* (New York: Harper, 1944).

13. On such self-operating "spheres of destiny," see Klaus Koch, "Is There a Doctrine of Retribution in the Old Testament?" *Theodicy in the Old Testament*, ed. James L. Crenshaw (Philadelphia: Fortress, 1983).

14. The point is clear in the famous declaration of Amos 3:2, in which chosenness provides no exemption but rather evokes negative attention from the divine judge.

15. A classic example of such a summons to civil society is the pressure exerted and the leadership provided by the church in New Zealand that caused the government, at long last, to honor the Treaty of Waitangi with the Maori peoples.

3. The Long, Slow Process of Loss

1. As concerns the reading of Scripture in light of the Holocaust, see the summary of Marvin A. Sweeney, *Reading the Hebrew Bible After the Shoah: Engaging Holocaust Theology* (Minneapolis: Fortress, 2008), 1–22.

2. See Jürgen Moltmann, *The Crucified God: The Cross of Christ as the Foundation and Criticism of Christian Theology* (New York: Harper & Row, 1974). For contemporary extrapolations on the cross, see Alan E. Lewis, *Between Cross & Resurrection: A Theology of Holy Saturday* (Grand Rapids: Eerdmans, 2001).

3. See the remarkable statement on the Book of Lamentations by Kathleen M. O'Connor, *Lamentations & the Tears of the World* (Maryknoll, N.Y.: Orbis Books, 2002).

4. Robert R. Wilson, *Prophecy and Society in Ancient Israel* (Philadelphia: Fortress, 1980), has shown how prophets at the "periphery" could make a case against the power arrangements, even though they are "irregular" and "uncredentialed."

5. The "seventy years" of displacement in ancient Israel (Jeremiah 25:11-12; 29:10; Daniel 9:2), a cipher and not an exact number, has as its equivalent in Christian tradition the void of Saturday. The seventy years is between old world and restoration, as Saturday stands between Friday death and Sunday new life.

6. It is worth notice that the term rendered as "vassal" (*mas*) is elsewhere often rendered as "forced labor." Recognition of this usage helps tie the poetic line more fully to Israel's recurring struggle with exploitative power. The downward reversal of Jerusalem in this verse has a parallel in Isaiah 47:1-3 concerning the reversal of the destiny of Babylon.

7. Tod Linafelt, *Surviving Lamentations: Catastrophe, Lament, and Protest in the Afterlife of a Biblical Book* (Chicago: University of Chicago Press, 2000), 45.

8. Ibid., 59.

9. A better rendering is "destroyed violently."

10. The ideology of U.S. exceptionalism lags considerably behind the facts on the ground. The rise of China and the resistance of Islamic culture to the democratic capitalism of the United States require a serious rethinking of that ideology. Because U.S. exceptionalism has a theological rootage, the matter is complex with reference to Islamic religious resistance.

11. See the pre–9/11 thesis of Francis Fukuyama, *The End of History and the Last Man* (New York: Free Press, 1992).

12. This view was boldly articulated by Steven G. Calabresi in a letter to the *New York Times*:

> Those of us concerned about citation of foreign law . . . believe in . . . American exceptionalism, which holds that the United States is a beacon

of liberty, democracy and equality of opportunity to the rest of the world. . . . We believe that the rights of man, as President Kennedy said, . . . "come not from the generosity of the state, but from the hand of God." The country that saved Europe from tyranny . . . in the 20th century and that is now saving it again from the threat of terrorist extremism and Russian tyranny needs no lessons from the socialist constitutional courts of Europe on what liberty consists of. (*New York Times*, sec. A, September 20, 2008)

13. F. W. Dobbs-Allsopp, *Lamentations*, Interpretation (Louisville: Westminster John Knox, 2002); Adele Berlin, *Lamentations*, OTL (Louisville: Westminster John Knox, 2002); John M. Bracke, *Jeremiah 30–52 and Lamentations*, WBC (Louisville: Westminster John Knox, 2000); Erhard S. Gerstenberger, *Psalms, Part 2, and Lamentations*, FOTL (Grand Rapids: Eerdmans, 2001); Kathleen M. O'Connor, *Lamentations & the Tears of the World* (Maryknoll, N.Y.: Orbis Books, 2002).

14. Scott A. Ellington, *Risking Truth: Reshaping the World through Prayers of Lament*, Princeton Theological Monograph Series (Eugene, Ore.: Pickwick Publications, 2008).

15. Nancy C. Lee, *The Singers of Lamentations: Cities under Siege, from Ur to Jerusalem to Sarajevo*, BibInt 60 (Leiden: Brill, 2002).

16. Linafelt, *Surviving Lamentations*.

17. Carleen R. Mandolfo, *Daughter Zion Talks Back to the Prophets: A Dialogic Theology of the Book of Lamentations*, SemeiaSt (Atlanta: Society of Biblical Literature, 2007). For an extreme statement of the alien work of God, see David R. Blumenthal, *Facing the Abusing God: A Theology of Protest* (Louisville: Westminster John Knox, 1993).

18. After completing a commentary on the book of Lamentations, the second half of O'Connor's book takes up, in more thematic fashion, all of the hard issues of violence, abuse, and nihilism that are commonly slotted under the rubric of "theodicy." But her perspective is one of pastoral compassion without any attempt to "explain away."

19. *Lamentations in Ancient and Contemporary Cultural Context*, ed. Nancy C. Lee and Carleen Mandolfo, SBLSymS 43 (Atlanta: Society of Biblical Literature 2008).

20. Kathleen D. Billman and Daniel L. Migliore, *Rachel's Cry: Prayer of Lament and Rebirth of Hope* (Cleveland: United Church Press, 1999).

21. Michael Jinkins, *In the House of the Lord: Inhabiting the Psalms of Lament* (Collegeville, Minn.: Liturgical Press, 1998).

22. Stephen P. McCutchan, *Experiencing the Psalms: Weaving the Psalms into Your Ministry and Faith* (Macon, Ga.: Smyth and Helwys, 2000).

23. Michael Card, *A Sacred Sorrow: Reaching Out to God in the Lost Language of Lament* (Colorado Springs: NavPress, 2005).

24. Patrick D. Miller and Sally A. Brown, *Lament* (Louisville: Westminster John Knox, 2007).

25. Kristin M. Swenson, *Living Through Pain: Psalms and the Search for Wholeness* (Waco, Tex.: Baylor University Press, 2005).

26. Ann Weems, *Psalms of Lament* (Louisville: Westminster John Knox, 1995); John O'Brien, *Cry Me a River: Mary's Tender Tears* (Athlone, Ireland: Children First, 2008); Lynn Domina, ed., *Poets on the Psalms* (San Antonio: Trinity University Press, 2008); Wesley Stevens, *Learning to Sing in a Strange Land: When a Loved One Goes to Prison* (Eugene, Ore.: Wipf and Stock, 2009).

27. John Witvliet, *The Biblical Psalms in Christian Worship: A Brief Introduction & Guide to Resources*, Calvin Institute of Christian Worship Liturgical Studies (Grand Rapids: Eerdmans, 2007), has made an important beginning in moving the Psalms back into the center of the worship of the church.

4. The Divine as the Poetic

1. On the reuse of old tradition in the season of displacement, see Paul D. Hanson, "Israelite Religion in the Early Postexilic Period," *Ancient Israelite Religion: Essays in Honor of Frank Moore Cross*, ed. Patrick D. Miller Jr. et al. (Philadelphia: Fortress, 1987), 485–508.

2. The courage of such voices calls to mind Amos 5:13: "The prudent will keep silent in such a time; / for it is an evil time." These prophetic voices were obviously not "prudent" in running risks for their utterance beyond the permit of empire.

3. YHWH's restless freedom is evoked in 2 Samuel 7:5-7, wherein YHWH refuses a temple because it will limit divine freedom. The endless effort in ancient Israel to institutionalize YHWH always has to do with the maintenance or curbing of divine freedom.

4. Notably the purity regulations and the details of temple construction read like memos. The precision of such texts tells against divine freedom that is characteristically given in narrative, song, and oracle. Thus the issue of divine freedom depends, in textual articulation, to some great extent on the use of different genres of literature.

5. I have earlier called attention to the prophetic use of "until" in Jeremiah 27:7, 8, 22.

6. Norman K. Gottwald, *All the Kingdoms of the Earth: Israelite Prophecy and International Relations in the Ancient Near East* (New York: Harper & Row, 1964), 302, observes:

> The arrogance of the foreigner so deeply felt by Isaiah and Habakkuk is expressed in Ezekiel as an affront to the honor of God, especially in the persons of the merchant-king of Tyre and the god-king of Egypt. Yet Ezekiel shares with Jeremiah an essentially favorable attitude toward Babylonia, which he too regards as the great imperial chastiser and pacifier of the nations. There are, in fact, no oracles against Babylon incorporated in the book of Ezekiel analogous to those appended to the book of Jeremiah. The prophet's political knowledge [of Babylon] was ample.

In fact, Gottwald overstates the parallel between Ezekiel and Jeremiah precisely because Jeremiah does have oracles against Babylon, as Gottwald himself recognizes.

7. Gottwald, ibid., 328, construes Ezekiel's expectation:

> This can only mean that the restoration of Judah was to take place under the aegis of Babylon. Nevertheless, why should he suddenly expect that Babylon would re-establish the Jews in Palestine? The answer may lie in the stabilization of the empire which Nebuchadnezzar managed to achieve in his last years. . . . It seemed a likely prospect that the aged Nebuchadnezzar would begin a program of rebuilding in the west. By returning the Jews to their homeland he could work for economic recovery in Palestine, and an effective buffer against renewed Egyptian adventures would be established at the same time.

8. Commentators notice the curious maneuver in verses 23-24. After the self-assertion of YHWH as ruler, these verses allow for a human agent, David, who will effect YHWH's new rule. In the end, it comes down to human agency, even though most of the rhetoric of the chapter puts it otherwise.

9. On the importance of this text for the hope of displaced Israel, see Jon D. Levenson, *Resurrection and the Restoration of Israel: The Ultimate Victory of the God of Life* (New Haven, Conn.: Yale University Press, 2006), 157–65.

10. The shaping of tradition in the two prophetic books is done very differently. The book of Ezekiel is shaped in self-conscious and symmetrical ways, with the entire last half of the book devoted to hope. By contrast the book of Jeremiah is quite complex, so that the primary hope texts occur in chapters 29–33, midpoint in the book. Perhaps the editorial outcomes of the two books reflect the horizons of the traditionists in each case, those in Ezekiel much more precise and exacting in this as in other matters.

11. See Walter Brueggemann, "The 'Uncared For' Now Cared For (Jer 30:12-17): A Methodological Consideration," *JBL* 104 (1985): 419–29.

12. On the connection between Lamentations and Second Isaiah, see Patricia Tull Willey, *Remember the Former Things: The Recollection of Previous Texts in Second Isaiah*, SBLDS 161 (Atlanta: Scholars Press, 1997).

13. See Christopher R. Seitz, *Zion's Final Destiny: The Development of the Book of Isaiah: A Reassessment of Isaiah 36–39* (Minneapolis: Fortress, 1991), 193–208.

14. The analogue between Babylon and Pharaoh, in the imagination of Israel, is clear in the way in which Bernhard W. Anderson, "Exodus and Covenant in Second Isaiah and Prophetic Tradition," *Magnalia Dei, The Mighty Acts of God: Essays on the Bible and Archaeology in Memory of G. Ernest Wright*, ed. Frank Moore Cross et al. (Garden City, N.Y.: Doubleday, 1976), 339–60, traces the Exodus theme in Second Isaiah.

15. Paul D. Hanson, *The Dawn of Apocalyptic: The Historical and Sociological Roots of Jewish Apocalyptic Eschatology* (Philadelphia: Fortress, 1975), 238.

16. The classic discussion of the rootage and tradition of these two priestly "pedigrees" is by Frank Moore Cross, *Canaanite Myth and Hebrew Epic: Essays in the History of the Religion of Israel* (Cambridge: Harvard University Press, 1973), 195–215.

17. See Robert R. Wilson, *Prophecy and Society in Ancient Israel* (Philadelphia: Fortress, 1980), 241–51.

18. I have stated the matter here as though the narrative is older than the prophetic exercise of imagination. It could well be that the influence moved in the opposite direction, from oracle to narrative. The matter is in any case complex and admits of no simple formulation.

19. See H. G. Reventlow, *Wächter über Israel: Ezechiel und seine Tradition*, BZAW 82 (Berlin: A. Toepelmann, 1962).

20. See Michal Fishbane, *Sacred Attunement: A Jewish Theology* (Chicago: University of Chicago Press, 2008).

21. See Wilson, *Prophecy and Society in Ancient Israel*, 231–51.

22. The point is even clearer if we consider the corpus of Genesis through 2 Kings as the "Primary History." Then it is clear that the traditionists gave "equal time" to the two trajectories, for the Priestly tradition dominates the first four books and the Deuteronomic theology the final five. The normative tradition did not want to choose between the two nor did they want to give excessive weight to either one of them.

23. For one accessible rendering of the pluralism of the biblical tradition, see Israel Knohl, *The Divine Symphony: The Bible's Many Voices* (Philadelphia: Jewish Publication Society, 2003).

5. Contestation over Empire

1. See Daniel L. Smith, *The Religion of the Landless: The Social Context of the Babylonian Exile* (Bloomington, Ind.: Meyer-Stone Books, 1989); Daniel L. Smith-Christopher, *A Biblical Theology of Exile*, OBT (Minneapolis: Fortress, 2002).

2. On the empire of Rome in New Testament perspective, see Neil Elliott, *The Arrogance of Nations: Reading Romans in the Shadow of Empire* (Minneapolis: Fortress, 2008); more generally see Stanley Bing: *Rome, Inc.: The Rise and Fall of the First Multinational Corporation* (New York: Norton, 2006).

3. See John Hill, *Friend or Foe? The Figure of Babylon in the Book of Jeremiah MT*, BibInt (Leiden: Brill, 1997).

4. See Walter Brueggemann, "At the Mercy of Babylon: A Subversive Reading of the Empire," *JBL* 110/1 (1991): 3–22.

5. On these chapters, see Alice Ogden Bellis, *The Structure and Composition of Jeremiah 50:2–51:58* (Lewiston, N.Y.: Mellen, 1995); Martin Kessler, *Battle of the Gods: The God of Israel versus Marduk of Babylon: A Literary/Theological Interpretation of Jeremiah 50–51* (Assen, Netherlands: Van Gorcum, 2003).

6. The verb translated "stir up" is a telling choice of terms, used often to characterize the willful effect of YHWH on public affairs (1 Chronicles 5:26; 2 Chronicles 21:16; 36:22; Isaiah 13:17; 41:2, 25; 45:13; Jeremiah 50:9; 51:1). The term serves well because it allows for impact but refuses to say how or in what way that impact is enacted; just right!

7. The tradition, in articulating the engagement of YHWH in public affairs, effortlessly uses a notion of "double agency" as a way of linking divine purpose and historical reality.

8. The classic biblical case of gloating over the fall of an abusive power is the poetry of Nahum.

9. See Donald E. Gowan, *When Man Becomes God: Humanism and Hybris in the Old Testament*, PTMS 6 (Pittsburgh: Pickwick Press, 1975), 45–67.

10. Patrick D. Miller Jr., *Sin and Judgment in the Prophets: A Stylistic and Theological Analysis* (Chico, Calif.: Scholars Press, 1982), has exposed the way in which divine judgment, in prophetic speech, is commensurate with the offenses committed. So far as I am aware, this symmetry has not been studied with reference to the Oracles Against the Nations, but the same principle is at work.

11. This realism was voiced in the United States during the Cold War in the face of the threat of Soviet nuclear weapons, when the slogan was "Better Red Than Dead." The antithesis of that is apparently voiced in the enigmatic formula of the state of New Hampshire, "Live Free or Die."

6. Departure from Empire

1. In the tradition the land of promise is nonnegotiable. On the mistaken categories of the Assyrians, see Isaiah 36:17, wherein the Assyrian seems to think that other lands can also be lands of promise. The phrasing

"a land of grain and wine, a land of bread and vineyards" sounds not unlike the celebrations of land in the tradition of Deuteronomy (Deuteronomy 6:10-12; 8:7-10; 11:10-15).

2. Barbara Green, "The Determination of Pharaoh: His Characterization in the Joseph Story (Genesis 37–50)," in *The World of Genesis: Persons, Places, Perspectives*, ed. Philip R. Davies and David J. A. Clines, JSOTSup 257 (Sheffield: Sheffield Academic Press, 1998), 150–71), has carefully detailed the way in which the artistry of the Exodus narrative serves to ridicule and minimize the character of Pharaoh.

3. On this pattern in the final form of the prophetic texts, see Ronald E. Clements, "Patterns in the Prophetic Canon," in *Canon and Authority: Essays in Old Testament Religion and Theology*, ed. George W. Coats and Burke O. Long (Philadelphia: Fortress, 1977), 42–55.

4. Jon D. Levenson, *Resurrection and the Restoration of Israel: The Ultimate Victory of the God of Life* (New Haven, Conn.: Yale University Press, 2006), has made a compelling case that the restoration of Israel to covenant and restoration of Israel to land are themes that cannot be separated from each other in the tradition.

5. See Bernhard W. Anderson, "Exodus and Covenant in Second Isaiah and Prophetic Tradition," in *Magnalia Dei, The Mighty Acts of God: Essays on the Bible and Archaeology in Memory of G. Ernest Wright*, ed. Frank Moore Cross et al. (Garden City, N.Y.: Doubleday, 1976), 339–60.

6. It is worth notice that the image of "highway" from Isaiah 40:3-5 is taken up by all four of the evangelists in the New Testament, suggesting that "the way of Jesus" is understood as the way home for the displaced people of God (Matthew 3:3; Mark 1:2-3; Luke 3:4-6; John 1:23). In all four Gospels the imagery serves the motif of homecoming.

7. Eugene D. Genovese, *Roll, Jordan, Roll: The World the Slaves Made* (New York: Vintage Books, 1974), understands that in the old slave South, it was the insistence of the black preacher that the slave cotton choppers did not belong to Whitey. It was this reality that kept dignity and sanity available in an unbearable context.

8. The contrast of "old self/new self" in New Testament texts concerning baptism makes the point of transformation clear (Ephesians 4:21-24; Colossians 3:5-11). See Philip Carrington, *The Primitive Christian Catechism: A Study in the Epistles* (Cambridge: Cambridge University Press, 1940).

9. Marie Augusta Neal, *A Socio-Theology of Letting Go: The Role of a First World Church Facing Third World Peoples* (New York: Paulist Press, 1977).

10. See Walter Brueggemann, *Sabbath as Resistance*, downloadable group study (2007) available at http://www.thethoughtfulchristian.com/Products/TC0176/sabbath-as-resistance.aspx (accessed June 11, 2010).

7. A Durable Metaphor . . . Now Contemporary

1. In addition to the works of Daniel Smith-Christopher cited above, see James M. Scott, ed., *Exile: Old Testament, Jewish, and Christian Conceptions*, Supplements to the Journal for the Study of Judaism 92 (Leiden: Brill, 1997). For a contemporary discussion of the theme, see Edward W. Said, *Reflections on Exile and Other Essays* (Cambridge, Mass.: Harvard University Press, 2000).

2. The song is from the album *Stumble into Grace*, a reflection on the contemporary crisis of our society and the resultant sense of displacement so widespread among us.

3. Psalm137, the best-known exilic text, is situated between the scattering and the gathering. On that place between, see "from there" in Deuteronomy 4:29; "in the land of their enemies" in 1 Kings 8:48; and "from . . . all the places where I have driven you" in Jeremiah 29:14.

4. J. Clinton McCann Jr., "The Book of Psalms: Introduction, Commentary, and Reflections," *NIB* 4 (Nashville: Abingdon Press, 1996), 1024.

5. The same sort of inventory of finery is recited in Isaiah 3:18-23 as is found in Jerusalem. In that case as well, it will all be "taken away" by divine action.

6. In parallel fashion, the self-indulgent extravagance of Israel is condemned in Amos 6:4-7, there as well a cause for an ending wrought by YHWH to such an indulgent society.

7. Martin Luther, "The Babylonian Captivity of the Church," *Three Treatises* (Philadelphia: Muhlenberg Press, 1943), 115–245.

8. Ibid., 120.

9. Kenneth Scott Latourette, *A History of Christianity*, vol. 1 (New York: Harper & Brothers, 1953), 489–90.

10. Regina Mara Schwartz, *Sacramental Poetics at the Dawn of Secularism: When God Left the World* (Stanford, Conn.: Stanford University Press, 2008), 19.

11. Ibid., 20. Quotation within is from Augustine, Letter 138, "To Marcellinus cum ad res divinas pertinent," Sacramenta appellantur. *Patrologia Latina*, vol. 33, ed. J. P. Migne (Parisiis: Excudebat Migne, 1841), 527.

12. Luther, "The Babylonian Captivity of the Church," 245.

13. Allen D. Callahan, "American Babylon: Days in the Life of an African-American Idea," *The Bible in the Public Square: Reading the Signs of the Times*, ed. Cynthia Briggs Kittredge et al. (Minneapolis: Fortress, 2008), 67–82.

14. The accent on "place" is especially prominent in the novels of Wendell Berry. His much-noted *Jayber Crow, A Novel: The Life Story of*

Jayber Crow, Barber, of the Port William Membership, as Written by Himself (Washington: Counterpoint, 2000), comes as something of closure to the sequence of novels of a farm community. The book is almost a dirge over the loss of place that has happened with the encroachment of an urban money economy. Or in this context, we might say, as a result of the encroachment of empire.

15. The boasting of Babylon is matched by the boasting of Egypt by the witness of Ezekiel: "My Nile is my own; / I made it for myself" (Ezekiel 29:3).

16. A boisterous, flamboyant critique of consumer shopping is offered by "Reverend Billy." See Walter Brueggemann, "What Would Jesus Buy?" *Sojourners* 36/1 (November 2007): 8–15.

17. In his study of the Exodus, Michael Walzer, *Exodus and Revolution* (New York: Basic Books, 1985), 149, has written of Egypt:

—First, that wherever you live, it is probably Egypt;
—second, that there is a better place, a world more attractive, a promised land;
—and third, that "the way to the land is through the wilderness." There is no way to get from here to there except by joining together and marching.

It takes little transposition from this characterization of Egypt to read it as Babylon . . . wherever you live! (Quote within is from W. D. Davies, *The Territorial Dimension of Judaism* [Berkeley: University of California Press, 1982], 60.)

18. See Ben C. Ollenburger, *Zion the City of the Great King: A Theological Symbol of the Jerusalem Cult*, JSOTSup 41 (Sheffield: Sheffield Press, 1987).

19. Miroslav Volf, *The End of Memory: Remembering Rightly in a Violent World* (Grand Rapids: Eerdmans, 2006).

20. See especially the imperative summons of Isaiah 51:1-2.

21. The obsessive remembering of empire is well exemplified in the stunning 2006 German film *The Lives of Others (Das Leben der Anderen)*, by Florian Henckel von Donnersmarck.

22. As I write of "fruit," I call to mind the older novel of Lillian Smith, *Strange Fruit* (New York: Harvest Books, Harcourt, 1944, 1972), a tale of vicious and covert racism. Because the plot turns on a pregnancy, it is possible that Smith has in mind the sexual interaction of the races, but she leaves the title phrase enigmatic. More broadly than Smith would have said it, the novel is about the strange fruit of empire, in this case, the empire of whiteness.

23. Reinhold Niebuhr has of course taught us all that it is justice and not love that could mark empire. We need not quibble about the possibility of empire when our own example is open to so much criticism.

24. The phrase is from Colossians 3:5; see Brian S. Rosner, *Greed as Idolatry: The Origin and Meaning of a Pauline Metaphor* (Grand Rapids: Eerdmans, 2007).

8. Doin' Time in Persia

1. In his study of the Oracles Against the Nations in Amos 1–2, John Barton, *Understanding Old Testament Ethics: Approaches and Explorations* (Louisville: Westminster John Knox, 2003), 77–129, proposes that these oracles, shaped as speeches of judgment, appeal to a broad understanding of international conduct: "It will be suggested that he was appealing to a kind of conventional or customary law about international conduct which he at least believed to be self-evidently right and which he thought he could count on his audience's familiarity with and acquiescence in" (p. 78).

2. See Claus Westermann, *Basic Forms of Prophetic Speech* (Philadelphia: Westminster, 1967).

3. See Jon L. Berquist, *Judaism in Persia's Shadow: A Social and Historical Approach* (Minneapolis: Fortress, 1995).

4. Philip R. Davies, *Scribes and Schools: The Canonization of the Hebrew Scriptures* (Louisville: Westminster John Knox, 1998), offers the pertinent data on the defining role of scribes and sages in the formative period of Judaism.

5. David Weiss Halivni, *Revelation Restored: Divine Writ and Critical Responses* (Boulder: Westview Press/Perseus, 1997), has proposed that Ezra received from Moses a wounded Torah text that needed to be repaired, so that it is Ezra who provided Israel with a completed Torah text. Concerning Halivni's work, see the commentary of Peter Ochs, "Talmudic Scholarship as Textual Reasoning: Halivni's Pragmatic Historiography," *Textual Reasonings: Jewish Philosophy and Text Study at the End of the Twentieth Century*, ed. Peter Ochs and Nancy Levene (Grand Rapids: Eerdmans, 2002), 120–43. Halivni, ibid. 144–51, responds to Ochs's commentary.

6. Joseph Blenkinsopp, *Ezra-Nehemiah*, OTL (Philadelphia: Westminster, 1988), 307.

7. Ibid., 307–8.

8. It is plausible to view this text and the act of prayer as a "hidden transcript" in the sense suggested by James C. Scott, *Domination and the Arts of Resistance: Hidden Transcripts* (New Haven, Conn.: Yale University Press, 1990).

9. The fixing of blame on failed intelligence as given in the text is echoed in the belated attempt of George W. Bush to blame policy failures on failed intelligence.

10. The renaming of the Jewish young men—Hananiah, Mishael, and Azariah—by "imperial names"—as Shadrach, Meshach, and Abednego—is of immense importance for the narrative and its intention (Daniel 1:7). It is most telling that at the end of the narrative, they are called, yet again, by their Jewish names (v. 19). On the function of bilingual practice in the book of Daniel, see the as yet unpublished paper of Anathea Portier-Young, "Languages of Identity and Obligation: Daniel as Bilingual Book."

11. Berquist, *Judaism in Persia's Shadow*, 227.

12. See Jacob Neusner, *From Politics to Piety: The Emergence of Pharisaic Judaism* (Eugene, Ore.: Wipf and Stock, 2003), who argues in the same direction as does Berquist.

13. Gerhard von Rad, *The Problem of the Hexateuch and Other Essays* (New York: McGraw-Hill, 1966), 292–300.

14. Leon R. Kass, *The Beginning of Wisdom: Reading Genesis* (New York: Free Press, 2003), 572.

15. Ibid., 613.

16. Ibid., 569.

17. Gerhard von Rad, *Genesis: A Commentary*, OTL (Philadelphia; Westminster, 1972), 408–11, reads the text without a trace of irony. Such a reading seems to me quite implausible. Carolyn J. Sharp, *Irony and Meaning in the Hebrew Bible*, Indiana Series in Biblical Literature (Bloomington: University of Indiana Press, 2009), 60, comments:

> Yet a fourth irony emerges as we consider the unsavory aspects of Joseph's character. His ruthlessness in dealing with his brothers may have been contained, but his subjugation of the Egyptians has far-reaching consequences for the Israelites living uneasily among them. Joseph's preservation of life in the short term, while viable for survival, nevertheless leads inevitably to the trauma of enslavement and the necessity of fleeing into diaspora in the wilderness. Thus as the plot moves into Exodus, the ironies move toward a further level of narratological complexity, writing and overwriting each other in an increasing density of silences.

18. Berquist, *Judaism in Persia's Shadow*, 228–29.

19. Jon D. Levenson, *Esther: A Commentary*, OTL (Louisville: Westminster John Knox, 1997), 16.

20. I make deliberate allusion to Thorstein Veblen, *The Theory of the Leisure Class* (1899).

SCRIPTURE INDEX